THE
HUDSON'S
BAY
COMPANY

George Woodcock

THE
HUDSON'S
BAY
COMPANY

CROWELL-COLLIER PRESS

Library of Congress Catalog Card Number: 78–109444

The Macmillan Company
866 Third Avenue
New York, New York 10022

Collier-Macmillan Canada Ltd., Toronto, Ontario

Printed in the United States of America

FIRST PRINTING

Contents

CHAPTER ONE

The King's Visitors

In the early winter of 1665, the old walled city of London, with its narrow crowded streets where the upper stories of houses leaned together and almost shut out the sun, was nearing the end of its long medieval life. For months it had been half-deserted, its inhabitants fleeing from the plague and the nightly rumble of the death carts. Soon the city would be destroyed almost completely in the Great Fire of 1666, the germs of the plague burning with it, and would be rebuilt, to the order of King Charles II, by the architect Christopher Wren. Only those who were too poor to flee or too conscientious to leave their responsibilities remained behind. One of the conscientious ones was Samuel Pepys, diarist and Admiralty clerk, who on November 30 noted with "great joy" that the plague was abating, since in that week there were only 333 deaths, against 6,000 and 7,000 a week in the months of August and September.

It was in this London that Colonel George Cartwright arrived at the end of 1665. Coming from New York, the ship on which he sailed had been captured by a Dutch privateer in mid-Atlantic, and its passengers had been put

ashore in Spain to make their way to England. Accompany-
ing him were two fur traders from New France, Pierre-Esprit
Radisson, a young man in his twenties, and Médard
Chouart, middle-aged, known more commonly as the Sieur
des Groseilliers and to the English as Mr. Gooseberry.

The arrival of Radisson and Groseilliers was cloaked in
secrecy. Even Samuel Pepys, an adept in the gossip of
London, did not note it in his diary, though later on he
became interested in the flamboyant pair of adventurers
and preserved for posterity Radisson's account of his adventures in the Canadian wilderness. And certainly there
was need for prudence, since what the two Frenchmen
told King Charles II when they were spirited into his presence at the plague-time capital of Oxford, was treasonous
to France and of great possible benefit to England.

It concerned the vast salt-water gulf, cutting deeply into
the Canadian North, which is called Hudson's Bay. Though
claimed by France, it had been deserted for a generation
because of the hardships and tragedies men had endured
there. Groseilliers and Radisson laid a plan before the
astute and needy monarch. Listening carefully, he approved
the scheme unfolded by the Frenchmen and placed them
under his protection. Though two years would pass before
Radisson and Groseilliers finally set sail for Hudson's Bay
in English ships, that day in Oxford they must have felt
as if the ambitions they had cherished for many years,
in the face of many frustrations, were on the brink of ful-
filment at last.

Both men were French by birth. So, at the time of their
arrival in Canada, the New France beyond the seas, were
most of its white inhabitants, for it was barely a generation
since Champlain had founded the tiny settlement of

Quebec. Médard Chouart, who came first to the valley of the St. Lawrence, was born in Touraine in 1618. He took his title from the parental farm—Les Groseilliers, the Goose-berry Bushes—which still exists beside the Marne, near the village of Charly. Radisson's background is more nebu-lous, but his father appears to have been a small landowner. The family came from the Rhône valley near Avignon, and it is likely that Pierre-Esprit himself was born in 1636 near the old Papal city. This would mean that he was not an actual subject of the French king, since Avignon was then part of the States of the Church, and remained so until after the French Revolution.

We catch a first glimpse of Groseilliers in New France through the letters of Mother Marie de l'Incarnation, the Superior of the Ursuline nuns in Quebec, whom he used to visit because she came from his native Touraine. He probably reached Quebec about 1640, but he first appears in history in 1646. Then, according to the Jesuit records, he came down to Quebec from Huronia, a cluster of col-onies among the Great Lakes where French missionaries were seeking to introduce the Huron Indians to the Chris-tian life. Three years later the missions were destroyed by the Iroquois, and the Jesuits martyred in their smoking ruins, but when Groseilliers was there, as a soldier or a lay helper, Huronia was a flourishing center of Christian zeal, and here the young Frenchman may have imbibed some of those wanderers' dreams which later governed his life. In 1646, the year he left Huronia, the Jesuit fathers were excited by reports of a "sea" called Winnebago (Lake Winnipeg) "by which" according to Marie de l'Incarnation "they claim to find the way to China."

After he returned from Huronia to Quebec, Groseilliers

was concerned for a time with other affairs and places than
the great wilderness in the Northwest. In 1647 he married
the daughter of Abraham Martin, known as Master Abraham, a river pilot on the St. Lawrence. Master Abraham's
little estate was to attain unexpected fame more than a
century later as the Plains of Abraham where in 1759 the
British conquest of Canada was assured. In 1649, Groseilliers returned briefly to France, dropping from sight until,
in July, 1653, he came back to the valley of the St. Lawrence
from Acadia, now known as Nova Scotia. There he stayed
with Charles de la Tour, governor of the province. Groseilliers' first wife was the widow of a relative of de la Tour,
and it may well be that the connection was the most important dowry she brought her young husband, for de la
Tour and his family had close trading connections with the
merchants of Boston, and even closer links with the Kirke
brothers, a family of Scots who in 1629 had captured
Acadia and Quebec and held them until 1632 in the name
of King Charles I of England. Sir David Kirke, who became
governor of Newfoundland in 1639, undoubtedly helped
the de la Tours in their struggle for ascendancy in Acadia,
and many years later his younger brother, Sir John Kirke,
was to play an important part in the lives of Groseilliers
and Radisson and in the early history of the Hudson's
Bay Company.

The story of the de la Tours contains some striking an-
ticipations of the later history of Groseilliers and Radisson.
When Kirke invaded Acadia in 1629, Claude de la Tour,
the father of Charles, was captured by the British and
shifted his allegiance to them for a promise of land. On
this occasion Charles de la Tour remained loyal to the king
of France, but later, after he in turn had been captured by

the English, he too came to terms with the invaders and was actually made a baronet of Nova Scotia. But of all the parallels between the history of Charles de la Tour and that of Groseilliers, the most tantalizing is the tradition, unproved but persistent, that between 1646 and 1650, while in exile in Quebec, de la Tour made at least one attempt to reach Hudson's Bay by sea. This is not impossible since he was busily engaged in fur trading during this period. If the tradition is correct, the likelihood is that Charles de la Tour first implanted in the mind of the Sieur des Groseilliers the thought of establishing a trading empire in Arctic seas.

When Groseilliers returned to the St. Lawrence, he settled in Trois Rivières, on the north bank at the mouth of the St. Maurice River, about halfway between Quebec and Montreal. It was the smallest of the three settlements of New France in the mid-seventeenth century. None was yet large enough to be called a town, for even Quebec had only a few hundred inhabitants, and Trois Rivières contained no more than thirty families, mainly farmers who cultivated the land along the neighboring river bank and returned every night to shelter within its wooden walls. It had been established as a fortified post in 1634, less than twenty years before Groseilliers arrived; but even then it was an important economic center of New France, for the St. Maurice River provided safe access into the country inhabited by friendly Indians, and as early as 1610 Trois Rivières was the site of an annual fur market. It was also the home of many famous *coureurs de bois*, or men of the woods who traded with the Indians, and who eventually carried out some of the most daring explorations of the American and Canadian West. Jean Nico-

let who reached Lake Michigan in the 1630s, and Nicholas
Perrot who explored the upper Mississippi in the 1690s,
came from Trois Rivières, and the Sieur de la Vérendrye,
who reached the Saskatchewan River in the 1740s, was born
in the little town.

In Trois Rivières the link between Radisson and Groseilliers was established. Groseilliers arrived in July, 1653, and
six weeks later, he married a widow, Marguerite Hayet,
whose half-brother was Pierre-Esprit Radisson. It is not
known when Marguerite Hayet reached Canada, but in
1646 she married her first husband, Jean Veron, Sieur de
Grosmesnil. Radisson claimed that he reached New France
in 1651, presumably to join his half-sister after she had
become established there.

No authentic portraits survive of either Groseilliers or
Radisson, and we have to use our imaginations to picture
them when they became brothers-in-law and their future
association was assured. Groseilliers was thirty-five, with
years of experience in the wilderness behind him and a
driving ambition to plunge farther into the unknown than
any other man. He was better educated than most of the
coureurs de bois and could write fluently, but he was also
a man of stubborn feelings—a proud individualist, resentful
of imagined injustice, with little urge towards loyalty. He
was a man of strong character and great physical power, yet,
compared with Radisson, he comes off as the duller man.

Radisson cut a flamboyant figure, even in the age of
Charles II and Louis XIV. Arrogant, boastful, he was a
plausible talker. He was also a resourceful woodsman with
a genuine understanding of Indian psychology, and a very
capable fur trader. For reasons which will soon emerge,
he and Groseilliers cannot have met—at least as brothers-

in-law—until 1654. Though barely eighteen, Radisson could already boast of a remarkable past.

In the spring of 1652, the year after his arrival in Canada, he and two young companions defied warnings that the Mohawk Indians were on the warpath and went duck-shooting in the woods near Trois Rivièries. Having quarreled with his friends, he spent the greater part of the day on his own; on his way home he came upon their mutilated bodies. Almost immediately he was surrounded by the Mohawks, who with customary capriciousness refrained from killing him. Instead they treated him indulgently, feeding him, painting him in their own war guise, and teaching him Mohawk words and songs. His captors took him to their village near Schenectady, where he was adopted by one of the families. For several months he lived as an Indian. One day he went on a hunting expedition with three of the younger braves and an Algonquin captive of the Mohawks. The Algonquin talked Radisson into killing the Mohawks and escaping. At night they smashed the skulls of their sleeping companions and made their way through the woods towards Trois Rivières, which was close by. While attempting to cross the St. Lawrence in broad daylight they were seen by a raiding party of Mohawks and recaptured. The Algonquin was immediately killed with great cruelty. Radisson was taken back to the village with some twenty other prisoners, including French women and children captured in the raids on riverside farms. He was tortured and forced to see his companions killed with all the complicated atrocities which the Iroquois could devise. He was sure that his own end would be the same: to die, after many mutilations, in a burning suit of birch bark. But his adoptive family appeared and remonstrated for him.

In the end, Radisson was released. All his nails had been pulled out and parts of his body badly burned, but he was alive. Indeed, the Mohawks took him back so completely that in the spring, after he had healed, he was allowed to go off on a war party with his "brother" and a dozen other young warriors.

Shortly afterwards, with another group of Mohawks, Radisson went to trade at the Dutch post of Fort Orange, on the site of present-day Albany. A French mercenary of the Dutch recognized him and led him to the governor of the fort, who immediately offered a ransom. But Radisson seems to have developed an affection for his adoptive family. In any case, he had no wish to join the Dutch but was hoping for an opportunity to escape to New France. So he refused the governor's offer. No sooner was he back with the Mohawks than he regretted his decision, and on October 29, 1663, he escaped to Fort Orange. The governor sent him to New Amsterdam, whence he sailed to Holland and then to La Rochelle in France, which he reached in the middle of winter. Finally, at the end of March, 1654, he left La Rochelle in a fishing boat which took him to the Gaspé shore of the Gulf of St. Lawrence. There he found an Indian craft which took him to Quebec and he made his way back to Trois Rivieres.

The great rivals of the French in the fur trade were the Dutch and English. In the Hudson River valley, the Dutch, and the English after 1663, had a water-and-portage highway into the interior that rivaled the St. Lawrence. The rivalry among the Europeans was paralleled by that between the Iroquois Confederacy, the formidable Five Nations, who lived to the south of the St. Lawrence, and the Algonquin and Huron tribes which occupied the valley of that river and the wilderness to the north. Except for brief periods of truce with the French, the Iroquois traded with the Dutch and the English, and the Algonquins and the Hurons with the French, so that, in a very shadowy way, European spheres of influence were marked out which later became the basis for political claims.

By 1654, when Radisson returned from his life among the Indians, the entire French population of New France was less than five thousand. Almost every adult male, from the governor to illiterate Norman farmers, had come to make his fortune in the fur trade. Even the religious orders, particularly the Jesuits, entered into the trade with enthusiasm. Until the eighteenth century, when agriculture was developed, the fur trade was the economic mainstay of the French in North America. In this New France differed from New England, where from the beginning farming and fishing were developed.

Material gain was not the only attraction, however. Both laymen and clergy had other reasons for challenging the wilderness. Most of the laymen came to escape from the old feudal society which existed in France. In New France the farmer was not a serf; he held his land under freer conditions than the peasants at home. Class distinctions loosened, particularly when gentlemen and commoners entered into life in the woods. The life of the *coureur de bois*— the Indian trader in the woods who hunted and trapped on his own account—had an irresistible attraction, and many men refused to be bound to life on the land. When the authorities became concerned over French title to the region, restrictions were put on travel into the wilderness in order to reduce the flow of men away from the settlements.

The restrictions were not entirely effective because they

conflicted with the colonists' other aims—spreading the Catholic religion and French rule over as wide an area as possible. The Jesuits' interest in the fur trade, and hence in new exploration, was to support their missions. The lay authorities were also anxious to push forward into the wilderness. They had two aims in mind. One was the old European dream of finding a sea route to China. The other was to assure French control over Canada by out-flanking the New Englanders who were beginning to penetrate west of the Appalachians. This aim was achieved when La Salle sailed down the Mississippi in 1682 and claimed the great river valley for the French king.

To a great extent official policy and the aims of the *coureurs de bois* went hand in hand, and conflicted with the other official aim of promoting settlement. For if imperial power demanded more territory, the fur trade demanded new beaver-producing regions. Conservation was unknown to the fur trade in those days. The Indians, armed with iron tools and muskets from the traders, sought out and destroyed the beavers' dams, drained their ponds, and broke into their lodges, where they slaughtered them indiscriminately. Region after region was hunted out, and the trade moved steadily west and north, until, long after French rule had ended, the fur traders reached the Pacific.

One other fact had a great influence on the fur trade in North America. Climatically, the Arctic does not begin at the arbitrary line known as the Arctic Circle. In Canada the true Arctic is defined by the tree line, which reaches the Arctic Ocean at the Mackenzie Delta on the northwestern edge of Canada (a latitude of approximately 69°) and runs southeasterly to Churchill on Hudson's Bay, approximately ten degrees or six hundred miles farther south. This marks the northernmost frontier of the beavers, which cannot live without trees. The northern forests were eventually discovered to be richer in beaver than any other part of North America. Richer in a double sense. Not only were there more animals but, in the intense northern cold, their furs were thicker and darker and hence more prized by the felters and hatmakers.

Groseilliers and Radisson were the first to realize that the richest trade lay in this northwesterly direction, and the journeys they undertook, separately and together, between 1654 and 1660, confirmed them in this conclusion. About these voyages there has been confusion owing to Radisson's claim, in the narrative he prepared in 1669 for the founders of the Hudson's Bay Company, that he accompanied Groseilliers on a journey into the West between 1654 and 1656. This cannot have been the case, since in 1655, before Groseilliers returned, Radisson signed a deed for the purchase of land in Quebec. It would appear, then, that he magnified his experience as a fur trader to impress his employers. In fact there were three voyages into the *pays d'en haut,* as the French called the hinterland, one taken by Groseilliers with an unknown companion, another by Radisson in a Jesuit expedition, and the third by Groseilliers and Radisson.

In 1654 a temporary peace was arranged between the French and the Iroquois, enabling Indians of the western tribes to come to Quebec for the first time in several years. When the Indians returned to their own regions, Groseilliers and his unknown companion accompanied them in order to discover the whereabouts of the friendly tribes dispersed by the various invasions of the Iroquois. They traveled along ways which were then unfamiliar but which later became the recognized routes of the fur traders—up the Ottawa River, across Lake Nipissing, and thence to the northern shores of Lake Huron. The territory as far as Georgian Bay on Lake Huron was already familiar to the fur traders and the Jesuit missionaries, but Groseilliers and his companion went on down Lake Huron to Lake St. Clair, and thence, at the narrows of Detroit, they crossed to Lake Michigan, sailing over the lake to Green Bay, beyond the known world of the fur traders in the 1660s. Here, while his companion went on into the Wisconsin hinterland, and may well have gained the upper reaches of the Mississippi, Radisson remained to trade furs and grow corn for the return. He met the Pottowatami Indians, who had never before seen a bearded man. He reached the edge of the Great Plains and saw the herds of bison. He heard of the Sioux nation, and seems to have come across the Crees, from whom he heard stories of the "North Sea" or "the Bay of the North"—otherwise, Hudson's Bay—and of ways by which it might be reached. Rejoined by his companion, Groseilliers returned by way of Michilimackinac to Lake Huron and thence to Quebec, accompanied by a flotilla of fifty canoes of Ottawa and Huron Indians. According to a florid Jesuit chronicler, the canoes were laden with "goods which the French come to this end of the world to procure," meaning, beaver furs. One account tells that Groseilliers and his companion each brought back furs valuing fourteen or fifteen thousand livres, equivalent to at least as much in present-day dollars.

The next year, in July, 1557, Radisson set out in the company of Fathers Ragueneau and Duperon to the Jesuit mission among the Onondagas south of Lake Ontario. It was a dangerous journey, for the Iroquois escort had lost seven men in a canoe wreck and they planned blood revenge for this mishap. They decided not to kill the French but attacked the Hurons who accompanied the party, killing most of them. Radisson's clothes were soaked with the blood of the first victim, and for the rest of the journey he was in fear until he reached the Jesuit mission where Syracuse now stands. Before long, he and his companions discovered that the Iroquois planned to kill them too. But the French gave a feast, feeding the Indians until they fell asleep from overeating. Then they escaped in boats which they had built secretly.

This was in March, 1658. Radisson returned to Trois Rivières, where Groseilliers, now captain of the town militia, was satisfying his contentious nature in a series of law suits. By August, 1659, when his name again appeared in the court, he was noted as absent, and his wife appeared in his stead.

He had left with Radisson one month earlier. Groseilliers evidently regarded the journey as something more than another fur-trading expedition. So, obviously, did others. Governor Pierre de Voyer d'Argenson refused to permit the expedition unless accompanied by his own men, and the Jesuits also wanted to send a representative. Groseilliers did not improve things by telling d'Argenson that "discoverers came before governors," so that he and Radisson, with an unnamed companion, were forced to slip out unnoticed—which was not difficult because Captain Groseilliers had charge of the keys to the settlement. Near the mouth of the Richelieu River they met the Indians whom they had already made arrangements to accompany. The voyage got off to a bad start the first night, when the third Frenchman cried out while dreaming of being pursued by Iroquois; the

Indians regarded this as a bad omen and he had to be sent back home.

The aim of the two brothers-in-law was to explore the regions still unopened by the fur trade and in this way to build the foundations of a family fortune. Their immediate direction was westward, but Groseilliers had not forgotten the great bay to the north which he had learnt about on his previous journey. They traveled the familiar route up the Ottawa River, across Lake Nipissing, and along the north shore of Lake Huron to Sault Ste. Marie. They ran into Iroquois and knew hunger on the way, but in Lake Superior there was whitefish in abundance and little danger of hostile Indians, and they traveled along the southern shore until at Chequamagon Bay they halted and built a crude fort.

Many of the Indians here had never seen a white man before, and their trade goods gave Groseilliers and Radisson an almost godlike aura. "We were Cesars, there being nobody to contradict us," Radisson remembered years afterwards. They encountered the Cree nation, and learned more about the lands to the north. Then they went southward with the Chippewyans or Ojibways into the forests of Wisconsin, wintering near Court d'Oreille Lake, a visit commemorated in the name of the modern village of Radisson. Here they lived through a great famine, in which many Indians died, until hunting became possible again. At the end of winter, the elaborately costumed Sioux came from the plains to visit them and to hold a Feast of the Dead in which seventeen tribes took part. After the feast, the two Frenchmen journeyed seven days westward to the Sioux encampment where four thousand Indians lived. Here they stayed for six weeks in the vain hope of gaining a peace between the Sioux and the Crees that would make the West safe for the fur trade. The ice was rotting when they returned to Lake Superior and crossed to the northern shore, where the assembled Crees welcomed them. It is not certain where the meeting took place, but it may be significant that the Pigeon River, later part of the canoe route to the West, was called the Rivière des Groseilliers as late as 1775. To this day a small stream in the locality still bears the name of Gooseberry River.

At this point in his narrative of this journey, written in 1669, Radisson asserts that he and his companion went by river and portage from Lake Superior to Hudson's Bay. There they spent the summer, supposedly departing when the winter cold set in. At the Bay, Radisson claimed, they observed many curious phenomena, including that old favorite of travelers' tales—sands hot enough to bake an egg. The episode has an air of unreality, and a mere calculation of the time involved makes it seem impossible. We know from Jesuit accounts that Groseilliers and Radisson were back in Quebec by August 19. They did not arrive on the north shore of Lake Superior until the breakup of the ice in April, they stayed with the Crees for a while, and merely getting back to the St. Lawrence was a summer's task. In any case, in the southern Bay, cold weather does not set in until late September and by then the travelers had long been home. The tale was in fact fabricated to sell their project to King Charles. But there is no doubt that they learned a great deal about the country between Lake Superior and Hudson's Bay, and they appear to have concluded that an approach to the Bay by sea would be infinitely less difficult than a canoe route through the rugged country, north of the Great Lakes.

They made a triumphal return to Montreal, with sixty Indian canoes laden with quantities of furs (variously estimated at between 140,000 to 300,000 livres in value). The cloistered Marie de l'Incarnation remarked that their arrival compensated the local merchants for losses incurred in recent fighting with the Iroquois; as she shrewdly added, "without commerce the country is worthless." But Governor d'Argenson was still angry that they had left without his representatives. Either to enforce the law or—as Radisson maintained—"to grease his chops," he imprisoned Groseilliers, fined both men, and then confiscated a large part of their remaining furs. Radisson was understandably reticent about how much this left them, but the subsequent acts of the two men leave no doubt about their feeling of extreme grievance.

Groseilliers sailed for France in November, 1660, to seek redress, but the king's officers put him off "with fair words and with promise." Realizing there was nothing to gain in Paris, he decided to lead his own venture to Hudson's Bay. On his way back through La Rochelle he arranged for a vessel to meet him off the coast of Gaspé, at the mouth of the St. Lawrence. He returned to Trois Rivières in August, 1661, and in the spring set off downriver with Radisson and ten voyageurs, announcing his destination as "the North Sea."

The plan miscarried—Radisson blamed Jesuit interference—and this decided the two brothers to seek out the traditional enemies of France. They went on to Cape Breton and eventually to Boston, where they were welcomed by the local merchants and immediately began to discuss how the profits of the northern fur trade might be diverted to New England. They remained in Boston almost three years. At first they aroused active interest, and by the spring of 1663 they had found a ship and set off northward, reaching Hudson Strait. There, the Boston ship captain, unaccustomed to the sight of icebergs, declared that his supplies would not carry them over the winter. Though so near to their objective, he turned back. Groseilliers and Radisson then secured from some merchants the promise of two boats for a voyage in 1664, but one of the ships was wrecked before the voyage began. Once more, Groseilliers plunged into litigation, emerging triumphant but without a ship to carry out his plans, since by now there was a Jonah look about his affairs which put off the canny merchants of New England.

But local New England interests, and the wider commercial ambitions of old England were different matters. This was the age of the venturesome merchants, when trade in the remoter parts of the earth was carried on by great chartered companies, and the political interests of kings were mingled with the financial interests of their courtiers. Already, massive corporations like the East India Company and the Levant Company had undertaken ventures from which, in those days before marine insurance, individual merchants would have shrunk.

Out of the efforts of Groseilliers and Radisson arose the longest-lived of all the chartered companies of the mercantile age, the only one that still survives. The idea for the company, though, probably originated with two courtiers, fresh from England, who listened to the story of the two *coureurs de bois* in the late summer of 1684. Colonels Robert Nicholls and George Cartwright were among four commissioners sent by Charles II to supervise the establishment of English rule in the old Dutch colony of New Amsterdam, rechristened New York in honor of James, Duke of York, to whom the rights of developing it had been granted. By this time Groseilliers and Radisson had become disillusioned with their efforts to reach Hudson's Bay from New England, and were talking once again of trying to secure the support of Louis XIV. Nicholls suggested that they should accompany him to New York, but eventually Cartwright prevailed on them to go to England. The New Englanders, suddenly fearful that a rich trade might escape into English hands, came forward with new offers of ships and assistance but, Radisson says, "wee answered them that a scalded cat fears ye water though it be cold." So it was that these two men of the forests found their way to England and into the favor of King Charles II.

CHAPTER TWO

The Adventurers of England

What Groseilliers and Radisson had to tell King Charles on that winter's day in Oxford must have been substantially the same as Radisson's later account in his narrative of 1669—that they had actually traveled by river from Lake Superior to the shores of Hudson's Bay, and that the Bay gave access to the richest fur-bearing regions of North America. This in itself would have been sufficiently exciting to hear, particularly since, by right of exploration, the English had a stronger claim to Hudson's Bay than any other European nation; the shades of such brave voyagers as Hudson, Baffin, Button, Foxe, and James formed a solid company against a single Dane, Jens Munck, and no Frenchman was known to have sailed into the icy gulf. But Groseilliers and Radisson offered a yet more tempting prospect—discovering the elusive Northwest Passage. Seven days' travel by canoe from Hudson's Bay one reached "the Stinking Lake" (undoubtedly Lake Winnipeg), and from there another seven days would take one to the "South Sea" or the Pacific.

It can be imagined how later fur traders, toiling for
months every year over the long waterways and portages
that took them to the Pacific at the end of the eighteenth
century, would have answered this. But it had all sounded
very practical to George Cartwright, who told Lord Arling-
ton, the secretary of state, that he "thought them the best
present I could possibly make to his sacred Majestie." Even
the scientific sceptics of the Royal Society were thrilled by
the rumors that found their way to London; the chemist
Robert Boyle heard that the party (transformed into "two
English and one French man") had actually gotten to the
"South Sea."

Charles II was probably less credulous than most of his
courtiers, but at a time when exploration and daring were
opening out the world wonderfully, the dream of an easily
navigable Northwest Passage seemed attainable. Explorers
finally proved two centuries later that such a seaway did
exist, though it was then totally useless for commerce. But
the shrewd Charles, clinging to the rags of absolute mon-
archy, saw in the prospect of fur trading in Hudson's Bay a
possible solution to two of his perennial problems.

He was surrounded by a court of ageing Cavaliers, loyal
followers of his late father in the Civil War, who had endured exile with him until his triumphant return in the
Restoration of 1660. They were now impatient for their rewards. He was also involved in a delicate relationship with his
royal cousin, Louis XIV of France, from whom he hoped for
help in his constant struggle with Parliament, without com-
promising England's national sovereignty or his personal independence. His foreign policy was astutely directed to
preserving a balance of power in Europe. Nothing seemed
better calculated to affirm England's independence than

supporting a venture into a region—America north of New England—which the French had begun to consider theirs to exploit.

So Charles received his visitors amiably, promised them a royal ship for their venture and arranged for them to be lodged in Oxford with a generous allowance. When the court returned to London, he sent them to his castle at Windsor. They stayed for three months and conversed with the king's grave and gallant cousin, Prince Rupert of the Rhine, who was noted for his scientific curiosity. In the spring they went on to London, and there their plans slowly began to take solid shape.

Groseilliers and Radisson soon discovered that even royal promises may be slow to fulfil. The king had offered a ship but—impecunious as he was—no equipment, and even the ship was difficult to provide, for the country was at war with the Dutch. Charles contemplated the creation of a company of private investors to back an exploratory voyage, thereby avoiding greater risk for the crown than the loan of a vessel. The task of assembling the nucleus of such a company fell to a relatively obscure courtier, Sir Peter Colleton, whose large plantations in Barbados gave him a special entry into the commercial world.

It was, at the beginning, a modest and almost furtive venture. Sir George Carteret, another courtier-adventurer, was involved, and so was Sir John Kirke, brother of the David Kirke who captured Quebec in 1629 and later assisted Groseilliers' friend Charles de la Tour. There were bankers like John Portman and Sir Robert Vyner, and graft-rich civil servants like John Fenn, paymaster to the Admiralty, and Francis Millington, one of the commissioners of customs. They advanced small sums for equipping an expedition.

But all of 1666, and most of the following year, went by with little achieved, and the end of 1667 brought a positive setback. Impatient at the delay in obtainng a royal vessel, Sir George Carteret bought the ketch *Discovery* on behalf of his associates, but the vessel was found unsuitable and was sold at a loss of seventy pounds.

At last, in June, 1668, the leisurely preparations drew to a close, and the expedition was ready to sail for Hudson's Bay. King Charles finally loaned the royal ship *Eaglet*. From Sir William Warren the adventurers had hired the *Nonsuch*, a former naval ship. Both ships were small by modern standards, though considerably larger than the twenty-ton crafts with which Martin Frobisher had set out to discover the Northwest Passage nearly a century before. The *Eaglet* was a fifty-four-ton ketch, forty feet long and sixteen feet in beam. The *Nonsuch* was even smaller—forty-three tons, thirty-six feet long and sixteen feet in beam. They carried goods for a season's trading, including a quantity of wampum—Indian shell currency—which Groseilliers had sold to the investors. The *Eaglet* was commanded by a naval officer, Captain William Stannard, and the *Nonsuch* by the New England master Zachariah Gillam. Groseilliers sailed on the *Nonsuch* and Radisson on the *Eaglet*, but the ships' captains were in full command of the expedition, with instructions to keep the trade goods in their charge and to give out no more than fifty pounds' value at a time. It was evident that the two Frenchmen were not fully trusted despite being under surveillance for two and a half years.

Now that plans had moved into action, the grander figures involved in the venture gave it their open protection. The letter of instruction to the two captains bore the names of Colleton and Carteret, and also those of the king's cousin, Prince Rupert, of his friend the earl of Craven, of his secretary James Hayes, and of the duke of Albemarle.

The captains were instructed to build fortifications when they reached the Bay, to guard against surprise, to trade cautiously with the Indians, to catch any whales, to look for minerals, and to send the *Nonsuch* back before freeze-up with whatever furs had been obtained. They were to keep in mind "the discovery of the passage into the South sea and to attempt it as occasion shall offer," and "use the said Mr. Gooseberry and Mr. Radisson with all manner of civility and courtesy and to take care that all your company doe bear a particular respect unto them they being the persons upon whose credit wee have undertaken this expedition." On the third of June the stay-at-home investors sailed down the Thames in a barge to cheer the departure of the two small boats.

Two months later, the *Eaglet* came limping into Plymouth harbor. She had proved too deep-waisted for the heavy seas of the Atlantic and, after her mast was lost in a gale, Stannard turned her back. Radisson had to spend the winter in London, waiting to sail the following spring. While he sat there writing the colorful, partly fictitious story of his earlier adventures, Gillam and Groseilliers had successfully crossed the Atlantic, avoided the ice of Hudson Strait, and continued down the eastern shore of Hudson's Bay to James Bay, which hangs like a U from the southern end of the great slanted U of the main Bay. On September 29 they cast anchor at the mouth of the stream which Gillam immediately named Rupert's River. A week before they had seen their first Indians and had traded with them before seeking winter haven.

At Rupert's River they hauled their ship on shore to

prevent damage by ice, and built a log house with a stockade. They called it Fort Charles. Later it was renamed Rupert's House, and to this day the Hudson's Bay Company still trades on the spot where Groseilliers first began to exchange the muskets, powder, and shot, the hatchets, needles, and trinkets, for the thick winter furs of the north. Three hundred Indians came to trade, and, since they were new to such commerce, Groseilliers was able to buy their furs for trifles.

The winter was long, and it was late summer before they could get away, for, though they left Rupert's River on June 14, they found the northern part of Hudson's Bay still filled with ice, and it was not until August 12 that they were able to sail through Hudson Strait for home. But they appear to have lived well. Beer, brewed from malt they had brought, was stored in a deep cellar. They found abundant game and fish, Gillam alone killing seven hundred "white partridges," or ptarmigan. There were no deaths among them, though Gillam complained, in an interview at the Royal Society, that "in returning they had found some trouble of the Scurvy in their mouths." It was not until the eleventh of October that they made landfall in England. Three days later their arrival was noted by the *London Gazette*, which reported that they "returned with a considerable quantity of Beaver."

A few days later Radisson returned from a second abortive voyage, and the brothers-in-law were reunited. After the *Eaglet* returned the first time, the adventurers petitioned the king for another vessel and were finally loaned another small craft, the *Wivenhoe*. With Captain Stannard in command and Radisson as supercargo, it set sail in May. But Stannard was either unlucky or incompetent, for, though the *Wivenhoe* reached Greenland, he was unable to get through Hudson Strait and returned once again with the exasperated Radisson.

This disappointment was counterbalanced by a private sale of the cargo of the *Nonsuch*, which brought in a respectable sum. The account books of the Adventurers are so imperfectly preserved that it cannot be said whether any profit was realized, but it is likely, considering the abortive voyages of the *Eaglet* and the *Wivenhoe*, that there was a net loss during 1668 and 1669. Yet the *Nonsuch's* cargo not only proved the claim of Groseilliers and Radisson that the sea route to Hudson's Bay gave access to North America's richest fur territory; it also convinced their patrons to continue their support. With the safe and prosperous return of the *Nonsuch*, the true history of the Hudson's Bay Company began.

Already, on June 23, 1669, while the ship's fate was still unknown, a group of the investors obtained a royal monopoly on trade in the northern parts of America. No sooner had the *Nonsuch* returned than they approached the king for a renewal of the grant. The new grant was more sweeping than before, conferring the exclusive right of commerce within the entrance to Hudson Strait, as well as mineral rights and title to the seas, straits, and lands in the area, all for the payment of two elks and two black beavers a year, to be delivered only in the unlikely event of the king or any of his heirs deciding to "enter upon the said countries."

This was only a working instrument intended to cover the provisional committee which had organized the venture. It was necessary to establish a company that would give a durable form to the monopoly. In 1667 the main partners in the venture had already recorded the shares they expected to subscribe, but it was the lesser partners who first began to redeem their promises by providing the funds for the first voyage. Altogether, some £4,720 was subscribed by the time the charter was granted, but it was some years before the original pledge of £10,500 was actually fulfilled. On such capital, minuscule compared with that of corporations like the East India Company and the Africa Company, the Hudson's Bay Company began the long career that would outlive them all to remain, after the demise in 1951 of the British North Borneo Company, the last of all the great chartered companies whose records embellished the history of the British Empire. It was many years before the capital was increased, and then it was done not by new investment but by increasing the value of existing shares. The Hudson's Bay Company, during its early days, perfected the art of living on credit, wisely preferring indebtedness to the bankers to the perils of the stock market.

Prince Rupert headed the Company of Adventurers of England trading into Hudson's Bay, chartered by King Charles on May 2, 1670. Altogether, it was a handpicked group of eighteen of his most influential subjects, including a prince and a duke, three earls or future earls, three baronets, six knights, three gentlemen, and one citizen of London, the goldsmith and banker John Portman. Others were later admitted, notably James, duke of York, who in 1672 was actually presented with a £300 share to gain the luster of his name, with an eye to the probability that he would eventually be the royal patron.

The charter established the Adventurers as a corporation whose affairs were to be managed by a governor and a committee of seven, with a deputy governor to act where necessary on behalf of the governor. All of them were to be responsible to an annual general court of the shareholders and subject to reelection by the general court. Prince Rupert was appointed the first governor, but the four peers were left out of active office and the committee consisted entirely of commoners, including that solid banker, John Portman.

The charter goes on for more than seven thousand words of grandiose language. Yet it is unlikely that the king suspected the true value of the grant made in the handsome parchment, with its gilt initials and carefully painted miniature of Charles II, which is still preserved in the Hudson's Bay Company's archives. He doubtless had in mind a few cold and distant shores to which Indians came down from the forests and barrens. Subsequently, the charter was interpreted as referring to all the land that drained into Hudson's Bay. This, it was calculated, amounted to 1,486,000 square miles—almost half the size of the continental United States—including large areas of Labrador, Quebec, Ontario, the present prairie provinces, and the eastern part of the Northwest Territories.

Later successors to the original Adventurers would rule in fact as well as in title over this great area, but that was far in the future. Now the "true and absolute Lordes and Proprietors" of Rupert's Land were concerned with setting up a subsidiary governor on the Bay itself. The committee was unwilling to confer this responsibility on either Groseilliers or Radisson, whom they still did not entirely trust. Nor were they satisfied with the arrangement on the previous voyage, by which the ships' captains had charge of affairs on land as well as at sea.

Their final decision seems a curious one, for they appointed as their governor on the Bay a prisoner in the Tower of London named Charles Bayly. Bayly is an enigmatic figure in the history of Hudson's Bay. He was a zealous Quaker who had been to Rome in an attempt to convert the Pope. He had written at least eight pamphlets on his beliefs; had lived in Maryland; and seen the inside of prisons in France, Italy, and England before finally landing in the Tower in 1663 on a charge of "seditious practices." What this long-bearded Quaker had that led a committee of Cavalier gentry and city financiers to appoint him their most important officer in the field is not recorded. All we know is that they requested his release, and he was freed on the surety of Sir John Robinson, lieutenant of the Tower and a shareholder in the Company, with the understanding that he would "betake himselfe to the Navigation of Hudson's Bay, and the Places lately Discovered and to be Discovered in those parts. . . ." Even the privy council showed a surprising solicitude for the prisoner's welfare, demanding that the Company should "assure unto him the said Charles Bayly such conditions and Allowances as may be agreeable to reason and the nature of his Employment." The king and his councillors had no intention of appearing to use cheap labor.

For the venture Bayly commanded in 1670 a vessel was built at the Company's expense. A frigate of 75½ tons, the *Prince Rupert*, cost about six hundred pounds. Zachariah Gillam commanded her and, again, "Mr. Gooseberry" accompanied him. The *Wivenhoe* was the second ship, commanded by Captain Robert Newland; Bayly and Radisson went with him. The ships sailed on May 31, staying together through the voyage. When they reached the Bay, Gillam took the *Prince Rupert* south to Fort Charles, and

Newland sailed the *Wivenhoe* southwest across the Bay to the combined estuary of the Nelson and Hayes rivers. This place, some six hundred miles northwest of Fort Charles, seemed admirably suited for tapping the fur resources of the more northerly forests, and it was intended to establish a fort there as the main post on the Bay and the governor's headquarters.

Gillam got to the Bottom of the Bay, as it was called, buried his beer, grounded his ship, and supervised the building of a log house which he himself helped to thatch with sedges. The activity attracted the Indians, and they set up wigwams around the fort. They brought in not only furs but also venison and fish, including sturgeon and salmon trout. Gillam and his men supplemented this with wild geese, which became a staple of Hudson's Bay traders. By October 12 the new house was ready and the house built in 1668 put into order. An oven had been made, too. The mate, Thomas Gorst, records that they feasted "at pleasure with venison pasty." With stocks of flour, peas, and oatmeal, and with malt to brew beer, they seemed well supplied.

All had not gone so well on the other side of the Bay. The very day construction had been completed at Fort Charles, while most of the men were away in the woods looking for firewood, the guards were surprised to see a longboat coming into the mouth of the river. It was the *Wivenhoe*'s boat. Radisson had come to report the chapter of disappointments that had befallen Governor Bayly and his party. The *Wivenhoe* had almost been wrecked on a shoal near one of the islands of Hudson's Bay, but had finally gotten off and made its way to a site on the Nelson River, which Bayly took possession of in the name of King Charles, naming it Port Nelson and ceremonially nailing the royal

arms to a tree. At first the situation seemed admirable. The
woods were thick with game—wild fowl, snowshoe hare,
and deer—and abundant with autumn fruit, including gooseberries, strawberries, and red currants. But no Indians came
to trade, and there had been a severe outbreak of sickness
among the crew of the *Wivenhoe*. Two men had died and
Captain Newland lay seriously ill. The rest had been too
disheartened to build a house or make preparations for
the winter and they had decided to abandon Nelson River.

The next day Gillam took a rescue party of seven men in
the longboat of the *Rupert*, while Gorst, with four others,
accompanied him in the longboat of the *Wivenhoe*. They
ran aground on the bar at the entrance to Rupert's River and
stayed there until the tide lifted them off in weather "so
cold that ye water thickened and stuck to our Oares while
wee were rowing." They arrived too late to save Captain
Newland, who died the following morning, but Gillam
sailed the *Wivenhoe* from James Bay into Rupert's River,
where it was hauled up beside the *Nonsuch*. Captain Newland was given a solemn funeral, the guns of his ship booming over the freezing waters. His crew settled down to a
wretched winter in wigwams made of old sails, since it was
too late to build another house for them. They made do
throughout the winter, trading with the Indians and tend-
ing the hogs and hens brought from England. On Christmas
Day they made merry, "remembering our Friends in England." There were no more deaths, only occasional cases
of scurvy. Late in January Radisson went off to explore
Moose River, across James Bay, and returned in the middle
of March with reports of pine trees large enough for ships'
masts; later, Bayly returned with him and traded with the
local Indians for beaver pelts. Meanwhile, at Fort Charles,

the spring came early, and on March 31 they sowed peas
and mustard seed; by May the mosquitoes were busy, and
on the twenty-second of that month the ice went out of
Rupert's River into James Bay.

The ships prepared to leave. Bayly's orders had been to
establish a permanent settlement, to maintain trade with
the Indians, and buttress the company's claim to the land.
Port Nelson had been contemplated as the site of the
settlement but it was not until many years later that York
Factory flourished there as the Company's great depot on
the Bay. In the spring of 1671 the many discouragements of
the winter had told heavily on the men, and when Governor
Bayly, following Quaker principles, sought volunteers for
the task rather than pressed men, not enough came forward.
Gorst, one of the few who did, thought Bayly should have
ordered the men to stay.

On July 1, 1671, the two boats sailed out of Rupert's
River. More than three weeks were spent in James Bay cutting wood for the return voyage and exploring the area,
where Bayly imagined he found the remains of Hudson's last
encampment. On July 24 they started for home, with Bayly
commanding the *Wivenhoe*. In October they cast anchor
in the Thames.

The Adventurers welcomed them with mixed feelings.
They were disturbed by Bayly's return, and disappointed
with the failure at Port Nelson. On the other hand, the
returns from the cargo were gratifying. Eleven thousand
pounds of beaver sold for £3,860, a particularly satisfactory
sum in view of the small capital invested. But the committee cannily paid no dividend. Instead they used the
money, and as much more as they could borrow, to equip
a more elaborate expedition.

Bayly was retained as governor. The two Frenchmen were to accompany him. In preparation, they went about making a selection of trade goods, including "one thousand biscay hatchets . . . two hundred fowleing pieces and four hundred powder hornes with a proportionable quantity of Shott fitt thereunto . . . and more two hundred brasse kettles sizable of from two to sixteene gallons a piece, twelve grosses of french knives and two grosse of arrow heads. . . ." Tobacco was included in the cargo, and, following the practice of the *coureurs de bois* who traded liquor for furs, 834 gallons of brandy were taken too. Three ships were sent on this voyage. The *Rupert*, with Zachariah Gillam again in charge, and the *Messenger* were to carry the trade goods and return next spring. For service on the Bay the committee bought a bark called the *Employ* for £126. Bayly was ordered to establish his headquarters on Moose River, and bricks and mortar for building a fort were included in the cargo. To prevent another shortage of labor, a score of men were hired to winter on the Bay.

Finally, the committee decided to clear up a "misunderstanding" on the part of the participants. They made it clear that the real adventurers were the investors at home; the actual traders were employees, forbidden to buy furs on their own account on penalty of forfeiting their wages. This should be borne in mind as we follow the history of the Hudson's Bay Company. Except for a brief period during the nineteenth century, the Company remained one of London investors who risked their money and paid other men wages to risk their lives. Sometimes bonuses were paid for good trading, and sometimes employees became shareholders through investment in the Company, but the principle of profit-sharing was not acknowledged. In this, the

Company's men differed materially from the fur traders who worked out of Montreal under both French and British employers. These shared in the profits of the trade and were accurately described as wintering partners.

The three ships left on June 22, 1672, and arrived in James Bay at the end of the summer. The winter passed uneventfully but profitably, so that when the ice broke in the spring, the *Rupert* and the *Messenger* set out for home with more than fourteen thousand pounds of beaver, which the committee sold for £5,300. The Company was prospering, but the committee waited another eleven years of steadily mounting trade before declaring a dividend.

Meanwhile, on the Bay, the era of permanent occupation began, its first years under the rule of Rupert as governor in London, and Bayly as governor on the Bay. Radisson went back to London with Gillam in 1673, but Groseilliers and Bayly remained, carrying out a series of explorations to consolidate the Company's position in the southern part of the Bay and to extend its trading range. In the *Employ* Groseilliers sailed to Port Nelson, but, though he went up the Nelson River as far as it was navigable, he saw no signs of Indians. He returned to find Bayly preparing for trouble. The chief of the local Crees warned him that a more distant tribe was being incited by the French to attack the Company's post but the attack never came. Bayly began to feel the effect of French competition, for the *coureurs de bois* had set up a post eight days' journey up Rupert's River and offered higher prices to the Indians. This placed Bayly in a quandary, since the committee prohibited bargaining, which left room for speculation and private deals, and set up a standard of trade, or standard price in beaver skins for every item. Bayly relaxed the standard price as far as he could and tried to evade the French by setting up a temporary post at Moose River in 1673. The next year his men opposed the planned transfer of the trading headquarters to Moose Lake, so he sent Groseilliers there in the *Employ*, staying to defend Fort Charles against a feared attack by the Eskimos. Again the attack never came and, when Groseilliers returned, Bayly sailed to Albany River and New Severn River, on the southwest coast of Hudson's Bay. He gathered few furs but established contact with the Indians, and in later years important posts were built in both those places. Half-starved and exhausted, Bayly arrived back at Fort Charles in August.

Bayly had expected to find the ships of the 1674 expedition, but there was still no sign of them. Stores were low, and he decided that if the ships did not come by September 22 he would set sail for England in the *Employ*, a desperate intent since Hudson Strait might become impassable before then. But Bayly faced the alternatives of starving at the Bottom of the Bay or braving the ice at the top, and, after two winters there, he chose the latter. On September 15, two days before he intended to begin loading the *Employ* with the remaining provisions, he heard the booming of guns in the Bay, and shortly the *Rupert* and the *Messenger*, renamed the *Shaftesbury* for the rising star of shareholder Lord Shaftesbury in the councils of the nation, dropped anchor off Fort Charles.

The ships brought ample trade goods and provisions. They also brought one William Lydall who had orders from the committee that Bayly should hand over to him his patent of office and all his papers and stores. There had been talk in London—probably originated by Radisson—

that Bayly was trading privately. Whatever the truth was
—and the committee's papers were too ill-preserved to tell
—the committee decided in February, 1674, to dismiss their
first governor on the Bay, appointing Lydall, who had
traded for furs to Russia, in his place.

The new governor made the most of the occasion. He
took possession of the fort with the colors flying, the drums
beating and the guns of the ships thundering salute. Bayly
accepted all this with fortitude, but less endurable was the
prospect of having to spend a winter with the man who had
superseded him. For the captains decided that it was too
late to attempt the return journey, and the two governors
prepared to face a winter together, their staff augmented by
the ships' crews. This strained the provisions, intended
merely for the wintering servants until the arrival of ships
the following summer. Instead of rationing the stores, as
Gorst recommended, Lydall handed them out extrava-
gantly, declaring, "if we starve, we'll starve together." He
very nearly brought this about. Bayly retreated to Moose
River and spent most of the winter there, turning the
trading post into the permanent fort he had been ordered
to establish. In the spring he had the satisfaction of learning
that one Hudson Bay winter had been enough for William
Lydall, who gladly handed back the patent of governorship.
Lydall sailed home with all the Company's men except
three who elected to stay with Bayly. Groseilliers also departed.

Whatever the committee felt on seeing Lydall again, they
appear to have accepted philosophically the continuation
of Bayly's governorship. He remained at the Bay four more
winters. When he was finally relieved in 1679, there were
accusations of inefficiency and poor discipline. Yet on the

whole the Company seems to have been well served by
its long-bearded Quaker governor, who consolidated the
groundwork begun by Groseilliers and Radisson. He established Moose Factory as the permanent headquarters of the
Company in James Bay. He set up a new post at the mouth
of the Albany River, so that by the end of his rule the trade
at the Bottom of the Bay was firmly established in three
posts. He appears to have maintained excellent relations
with the Indians. He even explored the possibilities of mining, reporting large deposits of "isinglass" or mica on the
eastern shore of the Bay. His trade returns were good. His
last cargo, brought out in December, 1679, fetched almost
£8,300, showing a progressive rise in the productivity of the
posts, two out of three of which he had founded.

He thus seems to have given good value for the meager
salary of £50 paid him until within a year of his final dismissal. The circumstances of his dismissal are curious,
since in 1678 the committee had quadrupled his salary to
£200. When he died early in 1680 their appreciation lin-
gered in the letter of instructions sent to his successor John
Nixon. In part Bayly may have been used as the scapegoat
for losses due to the unsatisfactory shipping arrangements
of the Company, for which the committee and the captains
appear to have been equally responsible. In 1676, for example, the *Rupert* was diverted to search for Busse Island
off the coast of Labrador. It was reputed to abound in
whales, walruses, seals, and cod, but the *Rupert* failed to
find it for the simple reason that it did not exist. That
year only one small boat, the *Shaftesbury*, reached Bayly. In
1678 the *Rupert* wintered in the bay as a guard ship, and
the *Shaftesbury* was wrecked off the Scillies on its homeward journey, with the result that the whole year's cargo of

furs was lost. Misfortunes like these were a regular part of the Company's experience during the early years, but they were bitter disappointments and Bayly may have suffered for them.

But there is another possible explanation for his departure. Bayly was, after all, a Quaker. There is no record of his ever being involved in violence—indeed he appears to have been easygoing, for his strait-laced successor complained of "licentiousness" among the Company's men when he arrived in 1679. These were times when the Company's presence on Hudson's Bay, and its air of success, were breeding resentment and rivalry in New France, New England, and at home. Its military Governor Prince Rupert and his associates doubtless thought that they needed a more forceful representative than Charles Bayly, the man of combative words and pacific action, who had been willing to leave the seclusion of the Tower to spend the last decade of his life in the exile of Rupert's Land.

CHAPTER THREE

Battles on the Bay

Until the Treaty of Utrecht in 1713, the French never recognized the rights of the Company or any other English traders on Hudson's Bay, and for more than thirty years before the treaty they kept up a state of war—declared or undeclared—along the shores of the Bay.

The defection of Radisson and Groseilliers had not escaped the notice of the French authorities either in Quebec or in Paris. In the years following the Peace of Breda in 1667, the French looked on with chagrin as the English venture in Hudson's Bay moved ahead. News of the successful return in 1669 of Gillam and Groseilliers from their first voyage reached not only Paris, but also, in embellished form, Quebec. There Marie de l'Incarnation announced that Groseilliers had received a reward of twenty thousand *écus* and also been made a Knight of the Garter, England's most distinguished order of chivalry.

Inevitably the French sought to counter the double threat of the English thrust to Hudson's Bay: the threat to their territorial claims north of the St. Lawrence, and the threat to their fur trade as the more accessible forests were depleted of beaver. The English fur traders' advance up the Hudson River in the 1660s was now aggravated by the presence of their compatriots to the north of New France, and the French in Canada began to feel encircled. Yet King Louis was anxious to avoid open warfare with the English, since he needed their benevolent neutrality while pursuing his aim of military dominance in Europe. Instead of fitting out a naval expedition, his minister Colbert decided to use a Dutch seaman, Van Heemskerk, who had sailed on the *Wivenhoe* when it failed to reach Hudson's Bay in 1669. Van Heemskerk, with three ships and a grant of all lands he might discover towards the North Pole and in the direction of the South Sea, sailed in August, 1670; he was back before winter, having failed even to make his way into Hudson Strait. The news of his attempt provoked a protest from England, and Colbert was not inclined to embarrass Charles II in his efforts to keep peace with France. Van Heemskerk was dropped.

Reasons of high diplomacy did not satisfy the French in Quebec, whose livelihood depended on the fur trade, and the priests joined the protests. The Jesuits were particularly disturbed by the appearance on the continent of Protestant traders, and when Jean Talon, the intendant of New France, decided to counter the English threat without involving the government at home, he chose to dispatch an overland expedition headed by a militant missionary.

Bayly and Gillam returned to Hudson's Bay in 1672 and were surprised and indignant to find the arms of the king of France nailed upon a tree outside Fort Charles. A month earlier, they would have encountered a party of three Frenchmen and eight Indians, headed by the tough old

Jesuit, Father Albanel, and the young Sieur de St. Simon. They were sent by Talon to investigate the British fort, open trade with the Indians, and claim the land for France. All this they had done, the Indian chiefs proving as compliant as they had been to Captain Gillam in 1668.

Albanel's party left the Bay before the English arrived, but two years later, in August, 1674, the Jesuit turned up again. He was starving and destitute, having been robbed by Indians, but he still carried two letters from the formidable Count de Frontenac, governor of New France. One was to Bayly, commending the good Father to him, a letter which the English later used to prove that the French authorities had recognized their presence on the Bay. The other was of a more private kind to Groseilliers, reminding him where his allegiance lay.

All that winter, while Governor Lydall and former Governor Bayly maintained their separate dignities at Fort Charles and Moose River, Albanel remained, nominally a prisoner, since he had trespassed on the lands claimed by the English Adventurers, but actually a guest able to influence Groseilliers at will. In 1675 Father Albanel, with Lydall and Groseilliers, sailed for England, where he was kept in a gentlemanly kind of custody by Sir James Hayes, one of the Company's committeemen. Soon he was allowed to cross to France, the committee paying his way, "for which kindnesse," as Hayes later complained, "he soon made ungratefull returnes."

As soon as he landed, Albanel reported that both Groseilliers and Radisson were willing to return to France, and obtained not only pardons for them but also inviting offers. Why Groseilliers and Radisson decided to accept the offers, leaving the Company in 1675, is uncertain. Their actions before and after the event rule out any compelling loyalty to the king of France—who in any case was not the king of Avignon-born Radisson. Radisson had done reasonably well from the English: in 1673 he was given a salary of £100 a year to act as the Company's adviser (twice Bayly's salary then for his arduous duties on the Bay), and he married the daughter of Sir James Kirke, who evidently brought a fair dowry. We do not know what rewards Groseilliers received, but they were doubtless comparable.

Radisson later claimed that they left because the committee rejected their advice with contempt, preferring that of "other persons," presumably Bayly and Gillam. It is likely, too, that they expected a greater share of the returns than they actually received.

Colbert promised, besides their pardons, to pay them 400 louis d'or, to settle their debts, and to provide them with "good employments." All was fulfiled—except the employment, and in 1676 Groseilliers and Radisson returned to Canada. There Groseilliers appears to have sunk back into the small-town life of Trois Rivières, taking up his interrupted career of litigation. Radisson returned to France and between 1677 and 1678 took part in an ill-fated expedition to the Caribbean. Shipwrecked near Curaçao, he was cast up on the gull-spattered island of Aves, losing all he had gained in the pillage of Tobago. He went back to London and tried unsuccessfully to get his wife to return with him to France. He was in England again in 1681 and for some reason warned the Company of dangers that the committee went on to outline to Nixon, governor on the Bay.

"We are informed by one Radisson a Frenchman who formerly served the Company," their letter said, "that the French have built a Fort and settled a Factory within lesse than a dayes Journey from Ruperts River, wch. if it bee true, our dangers from the French doe approach, *but however we knowe well our settlemt. in the Bay is a great offence to the French, and therefore it concerns us, to be careful to secure our Factoryes from any design of theyres or of the Natives* upon us, To which end we advise you that in all places *where your Factoryes are Established, you make some defensive Fortifications* as Capt. Guillam did at first at Rupert river, where hee digged a Graft and Strengthned with pallisades, and wee desire that Fort may bee repaired and kept in order by those which from time to time shall bee employed in that Factory."

This can hardly have been news, for before Bayly left in 1679, he was visited by the explorer of the Mississippi, Louis Jolliet. Jolliet spent two days with Bayly and later claimed that Bayly tried to recruit him into the Company with an offer of ten thousand livres and a thousand livres a year thereafter. The claim is unconvincing, since Bayly did not have the power to commit such sums, and Jolliet may merely have used the story to disguise other dealings with Bayly. For in the following year his brother Zacharie sailed to Hudson's Bay and on his return to Quebec was convicted of selling furs to the English and exchanging presents with the governor of the Bay.

Whatever their intentions, the Jolliets gave useful information about the English fort to the authorities in Quebec. Yet the French did not intervene until 1682, and then not at the thriving posts on James Bay but at unprofitable Port Nelson. There was an obvious desire not to provoke the English too far.

In 1682 the Hudson's Bay Company decided to establish a

fort at the estuary of the Nelson and Hayes rivers, to serve as a separate government seat from that of John Nixon on James Bay. The committee prepared to send out its largest fleet, two vessels to sail to Port Nelson and three to the new depot on Charlton Island in James Bay. Old Zachariah Gillam, who had not been employed by the Company for eight years, was given command of the *Rupert*, which led the fleet, and with him sailed John Bridgar, who had served under Bayly and now held the appointment of governor of Port Nelson.

The size of the fleet reflected the Company's expansive mood at this time. After more than a decade of meeting in taverns and coffee houses, the committee established a permanent office in Scrivener's Hall, which gave them the look of an established company rather than a loose group of adventurers. In a new departure on the Bay, Governor Nixon was instructed to send men into the hinterland to make contact with remoter Indians with richer furs, though the custom of bringing the Indians to the trade, rather than taking the trade to them, remained unchanged. Nixon was also instructed to seize all interlopers and send them to England for prosecution, a timely warning since no less than three sets of rivals were preparing to seize their share of the Company's flourishing trade.

One of the interlopers never reached the Bay, but involved the Company in difficulties for many years afterwards. In the early summer of 1682, a ketch named the *Expectation* sailed from Dartmouth, England, well stocked with trade goods and bound for the Bay. Hearing of its departure, the Company purchased another ketch, the *James*, equipped her with six guns, and sent her to intercept the *Expectation*. The *James* vanished at sea, but the *Ex-*

pectation had put back into Dartmouth, and wintered there, immune from seizure so long as she was outside the waters of Hudson's Bay. In the spring, repainted and renamed the *Charles,* she slipped out of Dartmouth harbor, reached Hudson Strait, and there was sighted by Captain Nehemiah Walker of the *Diligence,* one of the Company's roughest-tempered ship masters. After boarding her and imprisoning the crew, he helped himself to her liquor and put on board a prize crew which wrecked the ship on the rocks off Charlton Island. While he loudly claimed credit for putting an end to an interloping venture, Walker's action subjected the Company to years of litigation by the ship's owners, who claimed the *Expectation* had been captured on the high seas.

The *Expectation* was thus eliminated, but the two other interloping expeditions actually reached the Bay in 1682, to become involved in an extraordinary triangular conflict with the Company's men which ended in a triumph of French cunning over English and New English credulity.

The first ship to arrive was the *Bachelor's Delight,* out of Boston, commanded by Benjamin Gillam, nephew of Zachariah, and carrying as mate the appropriately named John Outlaw, later a servant of the Company and later still an interloper on his own account. The *Bachelor's Delight* put into Nelson River on August 19, and Gillam began building a post. The following day, unknown to the New Englanders, two small ships from Quebec put into the Hayes River, divided from the Nelson at this point by a marshy neck of land. Almost seven years after leaving the Hudson's Bay Company, Radisson and Groseilliers had secured support in New France for a trading company, the Compagnie de la Baie d'Hudson. With two small ships, the *St. Pierre* and the *St. Anne,* the French sailed about ten miles up the river, where Groseilliers went ashore to supervize the building of a small fort, while Radisson went on to establish contact with the Indians who, as luck would have it, were in the locality. While returning a month later Radisson heard the firing of ships' guns on the Nelson River. Proceeding there with Groseilliers and some of the Indians, he found the men of the *Bachelor's Delight* burying one of their companions. Pretending he was an Indian come to trade, he got aboard the ship before his identity was discovered and then told Gillam and Outlaw that he and Groseilliers had fifty men under their command (actually twenty-nine as against Gillam's thirteen). Radisson claimed that the land belonged to the king of France because he and Groseilliers had landed first (which was incorrect by a day), and he forbade the New Englanders—who could produce no title or charter of any kind—to trade with the Indians. If they complied, he hinted, the French would take them under their protection.

By a coincidence fit for an adventure story, Radisson was returning to his own post when he saw the Company ship *Rupert* sailing into the estuary. He went ashore but was seen from the ship, and the next day he and Bridgar had their first meeting. Again Radisson claimed that the land belonged to the French king, but the Company's men hotly disputed this, whereupon Radisson turned to bluff, talking of two ships, with a third expected, and three hundred Frenchmen up the Hayes River. The important thing was to keep the New Englanders and the Englishmen apart, for Radisson and Groseilliers knew that, if it came to a fight, they would unite against the French. But it never came to a fight, partly because of luck and partly because of

Radisson's clever maneuvers. He kept contact with each group without revealing the presence of the other, while Groseilliers guarded the fort and his son, Jean Baptiste Chouart, went upriver to insure that the Indians traded with them and not with the Hudson's Bay Company.

Twice luck played into Radisson's hands. The *Albemarle*, the second Company ship that was to come into Port Nelson, made first for Fort Charles and, because of its captain's death, did not come up the coast until the following summer. Then, on October 21, the *Rupert* was driven off shore by ice and foundered at sea. Zachariah Gillam died then and many of his men. Bridgar, with fifteen others, was left stranded without his ship, his artillery, and most of his supplies. He was virtually defenseless as long as he did not join forces with Benjamin Gillam, and he was dependent on Radisson for food to survive. For several weeks Radisson managed to keep the New Englanders and the English unaware of each other. Then, in February, when young Gillam learned by chance of Bridgar's presence, Radisson decided it was time to act. Taking the New Englanders by surprise, he captured the *Bachelor's Delight*, removed its cannons, and burned down the post Gillam had built. Before long Bridgar and his men were also imprisoned in the French fort.

The Frenchmen could be satisfied with their winter's work, but spring brought their first reverse, when breaking ice sheared off the upper parts of both their ships. They used the remainder of one to make the second navigable enough to carry the Englishmen, except Bridgar, down to the post on James Bay. Radisson and Groseilliers sailed in the *Bachelor's Delight*, leaving Jean Baptiste Chouart and seven men in the fort on Hayes River. They were to trade through the winter and await a ship in 1684.

The comedy was not played out, however. When the French party arrived with its prisoners and its prize vessel in Quebec, they found a new development in the ever shifting relations between France and England. James, the Catholic duke of York and heir to the English throne, was now the governor of the Hudson's Bay Company, Prince Rupert having died in 1682. Louix XIV was anxious not to offend him, and the victory on the bay therefore had to be represented as an unauthorized act. The prisoners and the *Bachelor's Delight* were released, while Radisson and Groseilliers were sent to Paris to answer for their inopportune behavior. Groseilliers returned to Canada and ageing obscurity; there is no record where or when he died. Radisson, only half willing, crossed the Channel to make peace with the Company and was received back with calculated forbearance.

Despite the setback at Port Nelson, the Company was bustling with activity. Nixon, grown old and morose, had been dismissed as governor in James Bay, and Henry Sergeant was sent out to replace him with an establishment which suggests that after only fifteen years of trading, the Company had begun emulating the East India Company. Sergeant was accompanied by his wife and a Mrs. Maurice. Somewhat disrespectfully described as his "parcell of women," they were the first English ladies to live on Hudson's Bay, and one can only admire their courage, particularly in view of the insults they endured on the long voyage from the irrepressible Captain Nehemiah Walker. The captain's behavior does not seem to have been tempered even by the presence of Mr. John French, M.A., the first English clergyman to serve on the Bay. To assist Mr. French in his duties, some five pounds were spent on Bibles, prayer books, and sermons. To assist Governor Sergeant, a secretary, three men servants, and a cask of Canary wine were provided. The Company meant to make an impression, and it did so most effectively by declaring its first dividend in 1684, an astonishing 50 per cent. The duke of York was paid in golden guineas presented in "a faire imbrodered purse"; ordinary stockholders received warrants on the goldsmiths, who were the bankers of the time.

The confident Adventurers took Radisson back in 1684, and sent him on the next expedition to the Bay. When young Jean Baptiste Chouart saw the white sails come gleaming into the estuary at Port Nelson, the final act of the comedy was played out. His uncle Pierre-Esprit Radisson had returned, but the ships were the English *Happy Return* and *Lucy*. Near Chouart and his companions was a group of Company men from the *Albemarle*, which had eventually reached Port Nelson in 1683. John Abraham had taken charge in the absence of Governor Bridgar but contented himself with building a fort, since he did not feel strong enough to attack the Frenchmen. Now that the balance of power had shifted to the Company, the Frenchmen's furs were seized, and Chouart and his companions followed Radisson's example by defecting to the Company. Abraham, though, distrusted them enough to insist that they be taken to England when the two boats departed in September.

Even without them, intervention did not end for almost twenty years. Only a week after the ships' departure, the help Chouart had awaited finally arrived, two small ships commanded by the Sieur de la Martinière. His instructions were confusing—avoid offending the English but also prevent them from establishing themselves at Port Nelson. De la Martinière appears to have been surprised to find the

English building a solid fort at a commanding point on the Hayes River. He attempted a night attack, which was repulsed by a cannonade, and then the rivals agreed on a winter's truce and lived amiably beside each other until the breakup. De la Martinière sailed for Quebec with the furs he had traded, leaving Abraham at the completed Fort York in command of the field. On his way back de la Martinière compensated for the winter's inactivity by capturing the Company's *Perpetuana Merchant*, an act of piracy which troubled relations with France for the next thirty years.

During the trading season of 1685 the Company had the Bay to itself, and Radisson functioned at Fort York with the resounding title of superintendent and director of trade. A new post was built on the Severn River, and, though the *Perpetuana Merchant* was lost that year by capture and another ship by wreck, two vessels did get through with satisfactory cargoes.

The duke of York had now become king of England as James II, and in 1685 he was replaced as the Company's governor by the formidable John Churchill, later duke of Marlborough. In the following year the Company embarked on a quarter century of embattled rivalry with enemies far more powerful than Radisson or de la Martinière. England was at peace with France, remaining so until James II was supplanted by William of Orange, but on the Bay a war began in 1686 that did not end until the Treaty of Utrecht in 1713, which confirmed the Company's hold on Hudson's Bay. The French claim was that the Bay was theirs and that a state of war was not necessary to justify action against the Company, which from their point of

view was an interloper. The English obstinately kept their
hold in the Bay because, they argued, the Bay was English
by right of exploration (Henry Hudson in 1610), prior
occupation (the erection of Fort Charles in 1668), and
by Gillam's treaty with the local Indians. Since the French
operated under the grant to the Compagnie de la Baie
d'Hudson in 1685, the conflict was theoretically between
two companies but the French who came to the Bay in
1686 had the active and material support of the governor
of New France, the Marquis de Denonville, while the
Hudson's Bay Company received little encouragement from
its former governor who, now the king of England, needed
French support to remain on the throne. Undoubtedly it
was James's weakness which led the French in 1686 to reverse their policy of restraint towards the English in Hudson's Bay.

The French sent an expedition to the Bay in March,
1686, a picked company of a hundred men, with five officers
and a chaplain, in a flotilla of thirty-five canoes. The commander was the Chevalier de Troye. Three of his four lieu-
tenants were sons of the Canadian landowner Charles Le-
moyne; they were the Sieur de Ste. Hélène, the Sieur de
Maricourt, and the Sieur d'Iberville. All the Lemoynes
were bold and intelligent; but Iberville's ruthlessness,
combined with extraordinary tactical ability, made him far
the most effective of the three. None of these leaders was
familiar with Hudson's Bay, but the quartermaster, Pierre
Allemand, had accompanied Radisson in 1682, and their
chaplain, the Jesuit Father Silvy, had made two journeys
there. The instructions from Denonville were clear: set up
posts at the mouths of rivers entering the Bay and seize any
interlopers; Radisson was named a specially desirable prize.

The Chevalier de Troye did not move against the English at Port Nelson, since de la Martinière's attack the previous year had put them on the alert for a possible new attack. Instead, the French objective was the posts on James Bay. Here the Company's officers felt so secure that when the French attacked Moose Factory at dawn on June 21 the cannons were unloaded and no sentries were on duty. The English, fighting in their nightshirts, surrendered after half an hour. A few days later the French force, with two small captured cannon, moved up the eastern shore of James Bay, to attack Fort Charles, and here again surprize was successful; the fort and the *Craven* were taken with little fighting. Among the prisoners were the perennially unfortunate John Bridgar, who had just been appointed governor, and Mrs. Maurice, one of the "parcell of women" associated with Governor Sergeant, whom Bridgar superseded.

The Chevalier de Troye now sailed to Albany, the strongest of James Bay's ports. But the spirit of the defenders was even weaker than the fort's wooden walls. After de Troye had carried out an hour's bombardment, John French appeared with a white flag on behalf of Governor Sergeant, whose wife had fainted when two shots passed through her dining room. The surrender was timely; the French were almost out of ammunition. By the nineteenth of August de Troye had returned to Quebec, leaving Iberville as governor on James Bay with forty men in his command. Iberville was ordered to send the prisoners back to England; instead he packed them into a small yacht with little food and told them to make their own way up the coast to Port Nelson. The Company claimed afterwards that twenty men out of fifty-two died of cold and hunger.

De Troye had certainly exceeded his orders by capturing

the English posts, and Iberville's hand may be evident here also. But the French authorities knew how to make a virtue out of disobedience if it worked to their advantage. To save the face of James II, the ministers in France proposed a treaty to end the strife. As concluded in November, 1686, it stipulated a truce based on the existing situation in the Bay. The French negotiators knew already of the capture of the forts on James Bay, but concealed it from the English, who did not get the news until February, 1687.

The company protested, advancing claims for damages amounting to £111,255, more than ten times its whole paid-up capital, but it never received compensation. Indeed, until William III came to the throne, bringing war with France in his wake, nothing was done to change the situation on the Bay, which meant that the Company was left with its fort at Port Nelson and its subsidiary post at Severn River, while Albany, Moose, and Fort Charles—or Rupert House—remained in French hands. Attempts on both sides to rectify the situation failed. In 1668 three Company ships reached Albany, but they were so outmaneuvered by Iberville, despite his smaller force, that by the spring of 1689 all of them had fallen into his hands, and he was using their trade goods to make up for the failure of his own ship to arrive from Quebec. But in 1690 when Iberville tried to round off his control of the Bay by capturing Fort York, he came up against the alert and aggressive Governor George Geyer and he was driven off, destroying the tiny post at Severn River in retaliation. Had he succeeded in capturing Fort York, the Hudson's Bay Company, deprived of its last post, would probably have gone out of existence after twenty years instead of surviving to celebrate its tercentenary in 1970.

As it was, the Adventurers, now almost entirely London merchants and financiers, showed an almost foolhardy optimism. In 1688 they declared a dividend of 50 per cent, in 1689 a dividend of 25 per cent, and in 1690 they tripled their stock, paying 25 per cent on the increased capital. They could do this in spite of their many losses because Fort York still sent good cargoes of furs. But the following year brought another long period of making do with expectations, for no dividend was paid again until 1718, after the French had finally departed from the Bay.

The twenty-five years after 1690 were, in fact, an anxious time. The Company faced not only French aggression in the Bay but also a shrinking market at home. By the end of the 1690s it had become difficult to sell large quantities of beaver in England and the Adventurers sought markets in Europe, while the traders in the Bay encouraged the Indians to sell them small furs, such as martens, rather than beaver.

At the same time a new breed of men had appeared among the Company's officers on the Bay, hardy men who had adjusted to life in the North and were beginning to show a spirit of daring like that of the French *coureurs de bois*. Henry Kelsey, who traveled far west to the prairies in 1690, was one of them. Another was James Knight, a carpenter and shipwright who became a great trader and the most dynamic of all the early governors. By 1692 Knight had twenty years' experience on the Bay, as craftsman, boatswain, trader, and eventually deputy governor. In that year he was chosen to lead an expedition to expel the French from James Bay. His resolution was such that he probably would have given a good account of himself anywhere, but circumstances played into his hands. Iberville, away on duty in the Atlantic through 1692, was unable either to

attack Fort York, as he had hoped, or to bring supplies to
Albany. The French at Albany mutinied and twenty men
deserted. When Knight arrived he found only five able men
and an imprisoned lunatic. He also found 31,000 fine furs
for the taking, and he was strong enough to beat off the
French relief ship that came in the summer of 1683.

From this time onwards the Company kept its three
trading posts at James Bay. The conflict shifted north-
westward, Fort York becoming the contested prize. Iberville
resented his defeat there in 1690 and wanted to wipe it
out, but his naval duties prevented him from returning until
1694. As so often happened in these campaigns, he then
won an easy and rather comical victory. Under George
Geyer, who defeated Iberville in 1690, Fort York had become a strong fortress. But his successor, Thomas Walsh,
was forced to surrender York to Iberville because he had
not stocked it with enough firewood. Iberville, with his
usual harshness, turned most of the prisoners out to face
winter in the woods, and many of them died.

Two years later the Company recaptured York. The
following year, in 1697, Iberville returned to fight the one
dramatic sea battle in the history of Hudson's Bay. Count
Frontenac, scourge of the Iroquois, was back in Quebec as
governor. He personally disliked Iberville as "a presumptu-
ous pup and a braggart," but recognizing the young Canadian as his best naval officer, he appointed him commander
of five ships sent out to sweep the British from the Bay. Iberville's flagship, the *Pelican*, was a forty-six-gun ship of the
line; the other vessels were smaller, with lighter arms. The
Company was already expecting French reprisals for the re-
taking of Fort York and—though neither side knew of each
other's presence—four English vessels, including the fifty-

two-gun *Hampshire* and two Company warships, the *Dering* with thirty guns and the *Hudson's Bay* with thirty-two, had passed through Hudson Strait less than two days before Iberville. One of the French ships was sunk by an iceberg. Aboard the *Pelican* Iberville lost touch with his other two ships and sailed across the Bay to Hayes River, expecting his consorts to join him. He anchored there on September 5, and the next day, when the English vessels came into sight, he thought they were his own. Realizing his mistake, he hurriedly pulled up anchor and sailed out to meet the enemy. In numbers and fire power, the odds were heavily against him: 3 ships to 1 and 114 guns to 46. But Iberville's boldness and skill made up for the disadvantage. The battle went on for four hours. The *Pelican* was raked by the British broadsides and suffered great casualties from musket fire; but, giving as good as it got, it kept the enemy from boarding. At one point, in the dramatic tradition of the old sea captains, Iberville and Fletcher, the commander of the *Hampshire*, pledged each other with bumpers of wine as gallant foes. It was Fletcher's last act. He fell in a volley of musketry. Then Iberville fired a decisive broadside and the *Hampshire* foundered with all hands. Soon the battered *Hudson's Bay* surrendered, and the *Dering* escaped to make its way home to England.

The battle had no sooner ended than a Hudson's Bay blizzard blew out of the northeast, driving the *Pelican* and the *Hudson's Bay* onto the beach. Many of the men were drowned trying to get to shore, but those who escaped reached the fort and reinforced its garrison. Iberville's two missing ships arrived, and with nine hundred men he laid siege to the fort. This time it was no quick and easy victory. The fifty-two men in the fort held out for four days, firing their cannon with an accuracy that alarmed the French and aroused their admiration. When Governor Bailey finally accepted the inevitable, he and his men were allowed the honors of war. They marched out, in the clear cold September air, with drums beating, flag flying, and their loaded muskets, matches lit, upon their shoulders. For once Iberville carried out the terms of the surrender, though he seized £20,000 in furs ready to be shipped to London.

At this point, as so often before, events in Europe intervened in the Company's fortunes. The French, English, and Dutch, having fought to a standstill in Europe, were all anxious for a brief respite. Almost immediately after Iberville's spectacular capture of Fort York, hostilities between France and England were ended by the Treaty of Ryswick. The negotiators had more momentous problems than the affairs of a small London company—no matter how large its territory—and, ignoring the actual situation in the Bay, they agreed to restore the status quo before the war in 1689. This meant that Fort York was to be returned to the Company, and the posts on James Bay to the French. It was also decided to set the boundaries between Rupert's Land and New France, but agreement was never reached and both sides clung to the positions they held when the fighting ended in 1697.

Fortunately for the Company—at least in the long run— the peace was short. In 1702, with the outbreak of the War of the Spanish Succession, Louis XIV and the English were again fighting. The committee, fearing a ripple of the war at the Bay, sent a second *Hudson's Bay* to protect its posts. They had cause for alarm, since the French had rebuilt the Severn River post between York and Albany and were active among the Indians in the hill country south of the Bay. The committee petitioned the government for three men-of-war and two hundred soldiers, but were turned down. Fortunately, the French could not spare any men or ships either, for John Churchill, the duke of Marlborough and former governor of the Company, was sweeping all before him in Europe. The tally of his victories—Blenheim, Ramillies, Oudenarde, Malplaquet—amounted to a decisive defeat for the hitherto unbeaten *Roi Soleil* (Sun King), Louis XIV.

Yet the war years were not uneventful on the Bay. In 1704 the French brought Indians down river to attack Albany, but the Company's men, now well trained, were on a constant alert, and the invaders were repulsed. A second attack in 1709 was driven off with "heavy losses." There were actually sixteen dead, but the French force consisted of only a hundred men and it was a high ratio. This was the scale of the fighting that decided the fate of the great Hudson's Bay region.

The worst effect of the war was the irregularity of contact with England. No ships were sent out in 1703 and 1704, so that by the time the *Hudson's Bay* arrived in 1705 to pick up the accumulated 51,000 skins, the traders there had been out of communication for three winters in succession. This involved less hardship than in the early days on the Bay, for the posts on James Bay, particularly Albany, were now largely self-supporting. Some of the Indians were now almost permanent employees of the traders, living near the posts—they were called Homeguard Indians—to fish and hunt in exchange for trade goods. By their efforts, and occasional shooting parties by the Company's men, a fair supply of fish and venison was available, while ptarmigan were abundant in the winter and wild geese were killed in large numbers during the migrating seasons. The supply of game was supplemented at Albany with some farm products, and hay was gathered during the short summer for the herds of hardy Orkney cows, sheep, and goats which had been introduced.

The Indians came to regard the Company's posts as refuges from famine. John Fullartine, a governor of Albany, reported that both there and at the small post established on the eastern shore of the Bay at Slude River, there was an "abundance of starved Indians," whom he fed "at least 16,000 fish, besides peas, oatmeal and geese." It was good policy for the Company's governor to look after the Indians he depended on for beaver pelts; yet there is a tone of real compassion in Fullartine's final comments:

> It was a very hard winter all over the country, for abundance of the poor Indians perished and were so hard put to it that whole families of them were killed and eaten by one another; the young men killed and ate their parents and the women were so put to it for hunger that they spared not the poor sucking infants at their breasts but devoured them. The reason of this famine amongst them was the little snow that fell so that they could not hunt beasts.

On occasions like these the Company's posts were a boon to the Indians. But in less desirable ways they were becoming dependent on the European and his wares. A Stone Age people, hunting with the bow, using knives and axes of flint or at best soft copper, and vessels made of birch bark, they took eagerly to the musket, the Biscay hatchet, and the brass or iron kettle. Within a few years they lost the art of making their own tools and weapons. So accustomed did they become to hunting with firearms that they completely forgot how to make or even use the bow. Such Indians were entirely dependent on the white men for a livelihood. It was more than merely a need for tools; many of the Indians became occupationally dependent on the fur traders, either as hunters and fishermen in the case of the Homeguard Indians, or as middlemen, neglecting the hunt to buy furs from more distant tribes and sell them to the Company. The profits on this trade among Indians were often enormous; Samuel Hearne in 1770 discovered that distant Indian traders were getting ten times as many furs as the Company demanded according to its Standard of Trade.

This pattern of dependence became more complex as the fur trade spread. When ships failed to come, the Indians suffered along with the traders. After three winters of isolation a post might be low not only on provisions but also on the powder and shot essential for the Indian's livelihood. At times Indians with furs to sell had to be sent away without desperately needed ammunition.

By 1705 the posts must have been extremely depleted, and the same must have happened to a less extent later in the war, for no ships went out from England in 1707 or 1709. Apart from the risk of losing its ships to French men-of-war or privateers, the Company was faced with great difficulty in recruiting at a time when the press gangs were active, and it was in perpetual need of ready money to fit out its ships. Albany and its lesser posts sent back excellent cargos—50,000 furs in 1705, 51,000 in 1711, 51,000 again in 1712—but during the war furs were easier to get than to sell, and it was only by risky ventures on the continent that the Company managed to make ends meet. These ventures involved it in new areas of business, for very often furs could be sold in Russia only by barter, and the Company might find itself with a shipload of potash on its hands or a cargo of hemp that would have to be sold at a loss to the navy.

Yet, in the long run, the bad market worked in the Company's favor. For bad as it was in England, it was infinitely worse in France, and the warehouses were piled with rotting furs. The possession of Fort York, or Fort Bourbon, as the French renamed it, became an embarrassment. During the war even fewer ships reached Bourbon than Albany, and relations between the French and the Indians deteriorated. In 1712 nine Frenchmen were massacred for violating native women, and the survivors dared not stir out of the fort. The French were so lukewarm about trade in the Bay that the Treaty of Utrecht's restoration of Hudson's Bay to the Company was readily accepted. The boundary of Rupert's Land was agreed as the watershed which divided streams flowing northward from those flowing southward into the St. Lawrence. There were delays in implementing the treaty, and it was not until the summer of 1714 that both sides were ready to effect the transfer of Fort Bourbon.

James Knight, who had recaptured Albany in 1693, was chosen as commander of the English expedition that would bring an end to the French presence on Hudson's Bay. He was now not only a stockholder of the Company but a member of the committee, and the first of that body to set foot in the land of which its members were "Lordes and Proprietors." He was to be governor of all the Bay, at the enormous salary in those days of £400 plus a commission on any new trade he might develop. He held a commission from Queen Anne as well as the Company. With two frig-

ates, the *Port Nelson* and the *Union,* he left Gravesend
on July 6, and arrived at Fort Bourbon early in September.
A French representative accompanied him, the transfer
went smoothly and politely, and on September 19, in an
official letter to the Company, Knight reported the re-
possession of "the whole country of Hudson's Bay and
Strait." French claims were thus liquidated; the Bay was
English once again, remaining so until in 1870 it was transferred to the new nation of Canada.

Fort York was in a state of decay when Knight took over,
for the French had not kept it up. In a more private letter
to Captain Merry, deputy governor of the Company, he
described the conditions:

> The place we are come to is nothing but a confused heap
> of old rotten houses without form or strength, nay, not
> sufficient to secure your goods from the weather, nor fit for
> men to live in without being exposed to the frigid winter.
> My own place I have to live in this winter is not half so
> good as our cowhouse was in the Bottom of the Bay, and I
> have never been able to see my hand in it since I have been
> here without a candle, it is so black and dark, cold and wet
> withal, nothing to make it better but heaping up earth about
> it to make it warm.

Like the Company's trade and financial situation, its
possessions on the Bay had suffered from the war, and a long
task of rebuilding lay ahead.

CHAPTER FOUR

Northern Explorers

When they left in 1714, the French ceased to exist as a force on the Bay. They returned in 1782, wreaking havoc briefly in the Company's forts, but they no longer laid claim to any trade or territory of Rupert's Land, and when the Hudson's Bay Company was defied in later years the challengers were rival Englishmen or—more formidable—rival Scots.

Sixty years, however, were to pass before the Company found it necessary to cope with Scottish competition in the form of the North West Company. The first half century after the Treaty of Utrecht was one of consolidation, peaceful trading, and relative prosperity. The Company was managed in England by solid businessmen of the City of London, who had replaced the courtiers and military men of its early years. In the lives of the earlier governors the Company was only one of many interests. But with the election as governor in 1712 of a lawyer, Sir Bibye Lake, an era began in which the growing affairs of the Company became the main interest of management.

In 1718 Sir Bibye paid the first dividend since 1690; it was a modest 10 per cent, but dividends were paid for every

year from 1718 to 1782, and then were interrupted for only
three years by a French foray in the Bay. He also initiated
a policy of investing part of the Company's income in gilt-
edged stocks, even if this at times meant negotiating short-
term loans for immediate expenses. In this way he diversified
and strengthened the Company's financial structure, so that
it weathered the stock market crisis of the 1720s and survived without harm the perils of trading in Arctic waters,
where no decade passed without the loss of two, three, or
even more ships by sinking.

There was only one disquieting gap in the Company's
security, and that a legal one. In 1690, after the flight of
James II and the accession of William and Mary to the
throne, the Company took the precaution of applying to
Parliament for the confirmation of its charter, and this had
been granted for seven years. In 1697 the charter came up
for reconsideration, and a number of rivals of various kinds
(including Radisson who was seeking a better pension from
the Company) tried to prevent its renewal. Hostility to
monopolies—especially monopolies granted by Stuart kings
—was particularly high, and it seemed certain that Parliament would vote down the motion to the charter. By obscure maneuvers of which no record survives, the issue was
allowed to die rather than be brought to a vote, and the
Company—neither approved nor condemned by Parliament
—reverted to its original position of a corporation chartered
by royal prerogative. On this basis it suffered in later years
a series of increasingly grave challenges. In 1749, for example, the Company's rivals forced the House of Commons
to set up a committee to enquire into its affairs and the
nature of its charter. However, Parliament decided that
there was no reason to interfere with the operation of the

Company, and a rival group which in 1752 sought a charter for trading in Labrador was refused, so that the Company retained its virtual monopoly of the fur trade.

Until well after the middle of the eighteenth century, the Company's trading policy on the Bay resembled that followed in the seventeenth century by the East India Company and other great chartered combines. A fort would be set up, staffed with traders and servants, stocked with trade goods, and the native hunters were expected to bring the furs there. One thing which Radisson and Groseilliers had not taught the English was the *coureur de bois* practice of taking trade goods to the Indians. It was a century after the Company started operations in the Bay that this was actually begun.

Life on the Bay was thus rather stagnant, and most of the traders rarely moved more than a few miles from their posts. One disillusioned Company officer of the 1750s, in a splendid phrase, called this period "The Sleep by the Frozen Sea." Actually, matters were never so stagnant as the officer, Joseph Robson, represented in his *Account of Six Years Residence in Hudson's Bay*, for there was increased activity along the actual shores of the Bay. The Company moved up the eastern shore, establishing a permanent post—Eastmain—on the Slude River, and in 1752 founded Richmond House farther north in the Eskimo region. But neither of these posts ever became so important as the one established at the mouth of the Churchill River, where the Company was attracted by the trade with the northern Indians and the whaling industry. Then, as now, the white whale came every year into the estuary in pursuit of the shoals of migrating fry. The first of the Churchill posts was established by James Knight in 1717, and shortly afterwards the committee decided to turn it into the main fort on the Bay. In 1731 Richard Norton began the construction of Fort Prince of Wales, as it was to be called. But he was no Vauban. He imported masons skilled only in building dry walls, and his ramparts were made of stone shells, cemented with clay and filled with hard-tamped gravel, so fragile that the vibration of their own guns would have demolished them. Later, in the 1750s Fort Prince of Wales was rebuilt into the massive, star-shaped structure of solid masonry which still stands on the river bank opposite to modern Churchill; it is the oldest surviving building in Canada west of Quebec.

Life on the Bay seems at this distance of time to have been hard and unattractive, yet there were men in the seventeenth century, as there are in the twentieth, who, after a few seasons on the Bay, found life at home insipid and constricting, choosing to spend the best and longest years of their lives in its bitter winters and mosquito-ridden summers. Such men may have been exceptions even then, but conditions on the Bay must be compared with the existence they might have known in Georgian England. By the early eighteenth century enclosure of the common lands was destroying the class of independent peasants in England; by the end of the century the crofters of Scotland were being forced off their land; and by the beginning of the nineteenth century the country people in both these countries and in Ireland were experiencing the acute want which William Cobbett angrily described in his *Rural Rides* and which in the 1830s led to great uprisings. For those thrust off the land, flight into the growing industrial towns was merely an illusion of escape; the realities they found were slum conditions and starvation wages in inhuman factories.

Those living on the seacoast, at any time up until the end of the Napoleonic wars in 1815, were also subject to the press gang, which might seize them for service on the king's ships, to live on salt meat and weevil-infested ships' biscuits, subject to ferocious floggings and even worse punishments which many did not survive. Life on the Bay, on the other hand, with at least a sufficiency of food and removed from tyrannical landlords, industrial regimentation, and high-handed naval officers, had its manifest advantages. It was also probably less monotonous than that of the average Englishman or Scotsman at home.

After the first generation on the Bay, the committee instructed the posts to become as self-sufficient as possible. This introduced great variety into the activities of the Company's men, who were encouraged to replace the Indians as hunters. In spring and autumn they salted down large numbers of wild geese and ducks; in other seasons, rabbits and ptarmigan. One post consumed ninety thousand ptarmigan in a single year. Catching and drying fish was on almost as large a scale, each post storing tens of thousands, and fish were caught with nets under the ice even after winter had set in. Caribou, moose, and deer were caught infrequently. The Company's men also took up trapping, particularly for small furs like marten, fisher, fox, or lynx, which the Indians rarely provided. These furs constituted a fair proportion of the annual cargo from the Bay to the London warehouses and auction rooms. At Churchill the men might even find themselves involved in the unsavory task of rendering the blubber of the white whale. Farther south, where rudimentary agriculture was possible, they tended swine and grew catch-crops of vegetables during the short summer at York. Radishes, lettuces, cabbages, turnips, peas, and mustard are among the crops mentioned in their letters.

In addition they gathered wild fruit, including strawberries and gooseberries, even as far north as Churchill. Dandelions were cultivated because they bore leaves early; indeed, this weed, abundant throughout northern Canada, is said to have been introduced by Hudson's Bay men at the end of the seventeenth century. At Albany, the farthest south of the Company's main posts, they reared their herds of hardy cattle and sheep.

It was wise as well as economical to rely as far as possible on foods grown or caught beside the Bay, for there were frequent complaints about the cheese, butter, and even salt meat from England. As late as 1786, the governor of York complained that a consignment of beef was rotten with maggots. Too much bad salt meat predisposed the men to scurvy, which remained a danger until the end of the eighteenth century, even though, from the first voyage in 1668, ships from England were equipped with lime juice and dried fruit. The scurvy was mitigated in later years by adopting the Indian custom of drinking a decoction of spruce shoots which provided the necessary vitamins.

Bread was made regularly, and beer brewed with malt brought from England. There were even experiments at distilling liquor for sale to the Indians as well as for consumption in the posts, but the rough alcohol was quickly abandoned in favor of West Indian rum or French brandy —this last available even in wartime from privateers.

For the general laborers, apart from food gathering and preserving, there were many tasks which varied with the seasons. The buildings had to be maintained, and this could be very arduous because of storms, ice, and spring freshets. Wood had to be gathered before winter set in, and ice cut and stored to preserve food and assure a supply of water. When the ships arrived from England, the laborers unloaded them and stored the goods in the warehouses, packing in sawdust anything that might be harmed by the cold. In between ships they dried, pressed, and stretched skins, and they gathered stones to ballast the ships, which came in heavy with trade goods and provisions and left with light cargos of furs. In the summer, the men at the posts manned the small craft which kept contact with the posts along the shores of the Bay, and they put out buoys when the water channels were open, and took them in before the freezeup. Finally, defense depended on the laborers. Considering that the only stake they had in the trade was their wages, they fought surprisingly well.

Each of the larger posts had its crew of specialists. The most important was the armorer, who not only kept in order the arsenal—cannons, swivel guns, blunderbusses, and muskets—but also cleaned and repaired the trade guns sold to the Indians. Often these arrived from England in an imperfect state and had to be put in order before the Indians would accept them. Indians who had lost the skill of hunting with the bow might starve if their guns were defective, so they became exacting judges of quality. Nevertheless, the Indians were slow to develop mechanical skill, and when anything went wrong with one of their weapons, they would bring it to the post for repair.

The smith was almost as important as the armorer. He made trade hatchets to supplement those brought in by the ships, and northern tools such as ice chisels; these were also made in England, but so badly that the governors on the Bay would often import iron so that their smiths could make chisels of the type the Indians preferred. There were also shipwrights, carpenters, and coopers, and even tailors. In later years surgeons and chaplains arrived, but these counted among the Company's officers rather than its servants.

There was indeed an elaborate pyramid of rank in a Company fort. It was an age that believed in the respect due to position and that this respect was best preserved by material signs of privilege. A rigid caste system was not allowed to develop, though. Men could start as artisans or even short-term laborers and rise to be governors at the Bay and even—like the shipwright Knight—members of the august committee that directed the Company's affairs from London. But this mobility was contrasted with definite distinctions between the various ranks of the pyramid.

At the head stood the governor of the Bay, with the deputy governor, the former usually earning £200 a year and the latter £100. Only the ship captains were their equals; a rivalry existed between the men of the posts and the men of the sea, though on occasion captains and governors would break the Company's rules by private trading. For brief periods there had been two governors, one at Albany and one at York, but after the recovery of York in 1714 it became the center of the Company's activities on the Bay and the seat of the governor. Chief factors or chief traders looked after the smaller posts, assisted by clerks who might earn no more than £10 a year and apprentices who earned only their keep. A chief factor at the beginning of the eighteenth century might receive £40 and a surgeon about the same, but later in the century these wages went up considerably. Gunsmiths, blacksmiths, and shipwrights occupied the highest rank among the servants; they were paid as much as £25 a year; carpenters and cooks a little less. The laborers were often hired on five-year contracts, their pay increasing towards the end of their terms to ensure that they would stay. In 1710 the Company began its long-sustained policy of employing Orkneymen as laborers. Their pay scale began at £8 for the first year, went up to £10 and then £12, and finished at £14 for the last two years. Since the men were also fed and received clothing and usually medical attention, their wages compare very favorably with those in England at the time.

The difference between men and officers was emphasized in the style of living. The governor might live in a primitive log building caulked with oakum, but he slept in a canopied bed, dined at an oak table, and ate off pewter plate, waited on by his own servant and attended by his secretary. He was allowed preserves and other delicacies to vary the monotony of the diet, and the Company's papers repeatedly mention presents of wine—a cask of Canary to Governor Nixon, eight dozen bottles of fine red wine to Governor Knight.

And yet, officers and men alike had to put up with the rigors of the Hudson's Bay winters. James Isham recorded in 1743 that ice six or eight inches thick collected on the inside walls of houses and was "every day cutt away with hatchetts." The rooms were dark with smoke from the wood stoves, and except for a few hours at midday the windows were covered with thick wooden shutters to try and keep out the cold. Even so Isham saw a two-gallon bottle of water freeze solid right beside the stove, while other accounts tell of brandy solidifying to the consistency of treacle. During the winter, the men wore their "toggies" or robes of beaver skin indoors, grew long beards, and rarely washed. Isham describes the typical fur trader as having at this season "a face as black as any Chimbly Sweepers."

The winter hardships were no worse than the agonizing boredom. In later years the forts of the fur traders maintained large libraries, but in the early days there was little to do but gamble and argue. Prayers were held each day,

and holidays like Christmas and Guy Fawkes' Day were
celebrated with the enthusiasm such occasions can arouse
among men away from home. Some tried to entertain themselves with music. But in the deep of winter, activity almost
came to a standstill, and it is surprising that violent disputes
were so rare among men cooped up in dark, smoky buildings.
The danger must always have been there, kept off by the
knowledge that a small group of men—rarely more than
sixty in number—could not afford to quarrel if they wanted
to survive the rigors of the weather and remain alert against
the continual possibility of attack by the Indians or the
French. Not surprisingly, Governor Knight, drawing up a
set of orders at Fort York in 1714, gave as his second rule,
"to live lovingly with one another not to swear or quarrel
but to live peaceable without drunkenness or Profaneness,"
and in his eighth rule again exhorted his men "to live
lovingly and do things with cheerfulness."

Drunkenness was a real problem and the committee
often emphasized the need to guard against it. Their anxiety
was justified, for the fort at Moose River was once burned
down at the height of a drunken party. Another recurrent
difficulty was women. The custom of establishing temporary
unions with them may have been introduced by Radisson
and Groseilliers, who lived by the morality of the French
coureur de bois. Though Knight warns against "jealousy,"
the Indians had no moral objection to such unions, provided they were formalized with gifts in the native manner,
and even the objections of the Company appear to have
been as much financial as moral, if we can judge from the
committee's instructions to Governor Nixon in 1682.

We are very sensible that the Indian Weoman [*sic*] resort-
ing to our Factories are very prejudiciall to the Companies

affaires, not only by being a meanes of our Servants often debauching themselves, but likewise by embeazling our goods and very much exhausting our Provisions. It is therefore our possitive order that you lay your strict Commands on every Cheife of each Factory upon forfiture of Wages not to Suffer any wooman [sic] to come within any of our Factories. . . .

Coming from the amoral London of the Restoration and Charles II, this was—to say the least—a surprising document. Its theme was repeated over many generations, but the most persistent efforts did not eradicate the practice of taking a temporary wife according to "the custom of the country." Even the highest officers on the Bay entered into such unions, which often created a bond—invaluable in trading and averting warfare—with the tribe to which the woman belonged. Sometimes such unions were happy and lasting.

During the tranquil period after the Treaty of Utrecht, the Company sought to solidify its links with the Indians, particularly from 1730 onward when French traders began competing with the Indian middlemen in the regions around Lakes Winnipeg and Superior from which many of the Company's pelts came. Trade inland was the only effective challenge; eventually the Company recognized this but at first it tried other expedients. One was to bind the Indian chiefs to allegiance by naming them captains or leaders, which gave them prestige, and by presenting them with gold-laced coats, three-cornered hats, and medals. The uniform Standard of Trade changed relatively little over the years—in 1684 a four-foot gun cost ten prime beaver skins, and in 1748 twelve—but the traders often had to depart from the standard to get any furs at all. Often, too, they had to use brandy or rum as freely as the French and adopt the custom of the regale, the complimentary drink with which trading began. But even before the end of the seventeenth century the Company's men realized the trade could not be maintained without extending the range of operation. Perhaps the most remarkable feature of the period Robson called "The Sleep by the Frozen Sea" was the extensive traveling, contributing greatly to exploration of the North and the West, which was undertaken by a handful of Company's servants seeking new sources of furs.

The first of these outstanding travelers set out as early as 1690, twenty years after the Hudson's Bay Company came into existence. Shortly after its foundation, the Company had begun engaging poor but educated boys as apprentices, so that it might build up a staff of young officers trained in the ways of the fur trader. In the beginning most of these boys came from Christ's Hospital. Some were completely unsuitable, but others took with enthusiasm to a new way of life, showing surprising adaptability. One of them was Henry Kelsey, who joined in 1684 and only three years later showed his mettle by carrying a packet of mail in midwinter two hundred miles from York Factory to New Severn—a task that had already defeated a group of Indians. "The Boy Henry Kelsey," said the Company, was "a very active Lad Delighting much in Indians Company being never better pleassed than when hee is Travelling amongst them."

Kelsey was one of the party that established the first post at Churchill in 1688, and the following year he set out on the first inland expedition undertaken by a servant of the Company. With the Indian youth who had accompanied him to New Severn in 1687, Kelsey sailed north from Churchill in the *Hopewell* about the middle of June.

They went ashore on the coast of Keewatin about sixty miles north, setting out "to bring to a Commerce" the Chippewyan Indians and the "dogside Nation," now called the Dogribs. Their destination was more than three hundred miles away over treeless tundra, and they were carrying not only personal necessities but also sample goods to entice the Indians down to Churchill. They were plagued by mosquitoes and drenched by rain, and in this land there was no wood for fire to dry themselves, to cook their food, or to make a smudge to keep off the mosquitoes. Traveling northwestward without seeing any Indians, Kelsey's companion finally became terrified at the prospect of meeting Eskimos. They had covered only about a hundred and forty miles but he persuaded Kelsey to return, which they did by a longer route that went through the haunts of the musk ox, which Kelsey was the first white man to encounter and kill. He got back to Churchill, after a trip largely by raft down treacherous rivers, a month and a half after setting out.

Kelsey brought no trade back but he had learned the indispensable lesson of living off the land as the Indians did. When George Geyer, the most enterprising of the early governors, wanted someone to send into the western hinterland, of which there were only vague accounts from the Indians, Kelsey, tough, knowledgeable and growing into manhood, was his obvious choice.

Kelsey's great journey into the west lasted two years, and he kept a journal of it in doggerel verse. He started off in 1690 with a group of Cree Indians who had been trading at York Factory. As before, his mission was to make contact with distant tribes, particularly the Stony Indians, and induce them to bring their furs to the Bay. He set up base at a place he called Deerings Point, probably near Le Pas to the north of Lake Winnipeg. Before freezeup, he traveled beyond the woodland into the great central plains, where he wintered with the Indians in their lodges, in a vain effort to persuade them to stop fighting and take their furs to the Bay. He was the first Englishman to see the buffalo and he was impressed by the grizzly bear: "mans food and he makes food of man." When winter was over, Kelsey returned to Deerings Point to pick up a parcel of presents sent out to him, and he headed west again in July, traveling fifty-nine days, a total of six hundred miles through the scrub forest and over the prairies until he eventually reached the Stony Indians and their traditional enemies, the Gros Ventres. Once again he failed to bring about a reconciliation in the interest of the fur trade. Although there are gaps in his account, it is certain that he took part in the buffalo hunts, then conducted on foot, for the horse had not yet been introduced to the Indians of the northern plains. Where his westward journey ended is less certain, for he did not know how to determine his position by the use of instruments. But it is unlikely that he got any farther than the Edmonton region, six hundred miles west of Le Pas, for he does not mention seeing the Rockies. He returned in the summer of 1692, accompanied by "a good Fleet of Indians," and the committee in London ordered that he be suitably rewarded.

Kelsey was not emulated for many years. During the next three decades the threat of French attack kept the Company's officers from undertaking any expeditions. Then, too, from 1697 to 1714 Fort York, the best starting point for journeys into the West, was in French hands. When peace came and York was returned, the Company began to think of resuming exploration, and in 1715 Governor James Knight sent out William Stewart to make peace between the Crees, who lived around the southern end of Hudson's Bay and were armed with trade muskets, and the less sophisticated Chippewyans, whom they had driven north onto the Barren Land.

Like Kelsey, Stewart traveled according to the custom of the country, accompanied by a Chippewyan woman remembered only as "the Slave Woman." She proved invaluable in communicating with her own people even after the Crees with Stewart shot nine of them, and eventually making the desired peace. During his journeys with the Slave Woman, Stewart was away for almost a year, traveling on foot like his companions and living off the land. He was the first European to cross the Barren Land, and did so only with the Slave Woman's help. Indian and Eskimo women were particularly skilled in the arts of survival in the North, and though Stewart often experienced the pangs of hunger, she enabled him to continue his journey even though many of the Indians dropped out. Unfortunately he left no journal, and we have to piece together his travels from Knight's laconic account to the committee. Stewart claimed that he went a thousand miles from Fort York, and, since he reached the northern forest on the western side of the Barren Land, he probably turned back somewhere south of Great Slave Lake.

Governor Knight was more anxious than any of his predecessors to increase the Company's knowledge of the North, and he seems to have been spurred by genuine curiosity as well as a desire for new customers. Immediately after Stewart's return he sent out another young apprentice,

Richard Norton, to encourage trade among the Chippewyans. This is the least documented of all the successful explorations undertaken by the Company. We know from Knight's records that Norton set out by canoe on July 18, 1717, together with a Chippewyan Indian and a "Young Slave Woman"—not Stewart's companion, who was now dead. It seems that Norton and his party traveled northward in the Bay by canoe until they reached the 60° latitude and then struck inland, returning to Churchill by a great arc through the hinterland. But where they went and what happened to them is unknown, though they are said to have undergone great suffering from starvation.

Even less is known of the journey on which Governor Knight disappeared from men's knowledge. Like many men of his time, Knight dreamed of discovering the mythical Strait of Anian—the Northwest Passage to China. He was also possessed by the desire for gold. He had seen specimens of the copper found far to the northwest, near the Arctic Ocean; the Eskimos and the Copper Indians used copper to tip their arrows and make knives. He had also heard rumors of another yellow metal in the same region; what could it be, he asked himself and everyone he talked to, but gold?

When he returned to London in 1718, he talked the committee into underwriting a voyage up the western Bay to find the rumored gold and the legendary Strait of Anian, insisting, though he was already seventy, on leading it himself. A frigate, the *Albany*, and a small sloop, the *Discovery*, departed from London in June, 1719, in the company of the regular supply ship, which they were to leave on entering the Bay. Then they were to explore the western shore up to 64° north.

The fleet set out and passed through Hudson Strait. The supply ship headed south, and from that point nothing was heard of the other two ships. By the time the committee in London began enquiring anxiously about Knight, it was evident that disaster had struck. Kelsey, traveling up the coast in 1721, and Captain Scroggs in 1722, established that the *Albany* and the *Discovery* had been wrecked on Marble Island off the entrance to Rankin Inlet. It was first thought that the Englishmen had been massacred by the Eskimos but information that Samuel Hearne later gathered from the Eskimos suggested that Knight and his men had died of starvation and scurvy. To this day the Eskimos of Rankin Inlet, when visiting Marble Island, crawl on hands and knees up its narrow beach in deference to the unhappy spirits of these long-dead searchers for the Strait of Anian.

For a long time Knight's disaster discouraged further exploration, until a fanatical believer in the Northwest Passage and opponent of monopoly, Arthur Dobbs, accused the Company in scurrilous pamphlets of failing to undertake the obligations in its charter. To stifle the criticism, it sent a small expedition to explore the western coast of the Bay, but with little result. A number of other voyages were undertaken, some financed by Dobbs and his associates, some by the Company. Their results were no more dramatic, though both shores of the Bay were charted fairly thoroughly by 1750, and it was proved that Chesterfield Inlet, on which the advocates of the Passage hung their hopes, led only to fresh water at Baker Lake in the heart of the Barren Land.

It was on land that the most remarkable journeys were undertaken in the years after Knight's death. Anthony Henday traveled to the Blackfoot country in 1754, and Samuel Hearne to the Arctic Ocean in 1770. Partly, these journeys were intended to offset French competition, which was particularly strong on the Albany River. Here, in 1743, James Isbister, a tough trader like Kelsey and Knight, took trade inland for the first time. A hundred and twenty miles up the Albany River he established Henley House, the first Company post in the interior. It was an ill-fated place, twice burned down and its men massacred by Indians incited by the French. But the Company kept rebuilding it, and though thirty years passed before another inland post was built, Henley House was concrete acknowledgment that the Company was beginning to accept the policy of going to the Indians who would not come to them, as the traders from Montreal had always done.

In keeping Henley House supplied, the Company's men were having their first experience of canoe travel and of packing their trade goods inland and their furs out. Meanwhile, the French were advancing westward. In 1731 the greatest of French fur traders, the Sieur de la Vérendrye, began to explore the Saskatchewan River and the rich fur regions that lay along its shores. This cut into the Company's trade down the Nelson and Hayes rivers to Fort York, and in 1754 Antony Henday left York on the journey to the western Indians that would make him the first European to set eyes on the Rocky Mountains.

Henday's journal is much more precise than Kelsey's rhyming diary, and we can trace his travels with some detail. After many portages, he reached Le Pas by July 22, where he found the French already installed across the routes followed by Indians who traded with the Company. Henday went on and west of Le Pas he left the rivers to travel overland with his Assiniboine companions. He reached the prairies, passed near the present sites of Saskatoon and Battleford, and about fifty miles south of the naked prairie that became Edmonton he reached the foothills of the

Rockies. This was the end of September. On October 1 seven handsome Indians in elaborate buckskins rode up to Henday's camp. They were Bloods, members of the great Blackfoot Confederacy which ruled the foothills. The next few days Henday traveled southwest, often passing through great herds of buffalo, until he came to the confederacy's main camp, with two hundred tents. The chiefs were impeccably hospitable, smoking the calumet with Henday, and feasting him and his party. But he was unable to persuade them to trade with the Bay. The buffalo herds gave them everything they needed: food, skins for clothing and shelter, horn and bone for weapons, sinews for thread, and dung—or buffalo chips—for fuel. On the other hand, they had heard, many of the Indians who attempted the journey to the Bay starved on the way. Besides, they would have to travel by canoe, to which they were unaccustomed, and to eat fish, which they did not relish. They preferred to remain as they were, and one has the feeling, from the tone in which Henday described the meeting, that in his heart he did not disapprove.

The Blackfoot rode away, leaving Henday and his companions to hunt among the foothills until, on December 24, they saw the Rockies for the last time and started on the slow eastward return. On April 8 Henday gave away his horse; he had come to the country of woods and rivers. On April 23 he unfurled a flag in observance of St. George's Day and shot a migrating swan with his bow. On April 28 the rivers were free enough of ice for him to set out for home by water and portage. As he went Indian canoes joined his party. Somewhere on the way, the Blackfoot brought furs to trade with him but refused to accompany him to the Bay. Twice French traders enticed the Indians to give up furs for brandy, but on June 20 Fort York's guns boomed out to welcome his return with a flotilla of seventy canoes he had managed to get past the French.

Not until the present century were the journals of Kelsey and Henday discovered and their importance as the first explorers of the Canadian prairies and the foothills of the Rockies acknowledged. Samuel Hearne, on the other hand, was hailed in his own lifetime for his splendid narrative *A Journey to the Northern Ocean,* one of the classics of North American travel. Hearne was a seaman who spent two years as mate on the whaling sloops that cruised up the western Bay. He had very little knowledge of the Indians when, in 1769, he was asked to undertake an expedition—another attempt to discover the elusive Northwest Passage and the rumored rich copper mines somewhere to the Northwest. Hearne was to accompany a trading party of Indians returning to the Barren Land and attempt to reach the Arctic Ocean, where the copper was thought to be. He was to claim the Arctic rivers for the Company, and gather whatever information he could about the Northwest Passage. Hearne was equipped with instruments to determine his positions in the still unmapped North. He had also a naturally curious mind with a wide interest in topographical and anthropological information.

Hearne made two abortive starts because of the rascality of the Indians with whom he set out. Then, on his way back from his second journey, robbed and starving, he encountered an extraordinary Indian, Mattonabee, who promised to go with him on a third attempt and provide plenty of women to carry the burdens and perform a variety of other necessary tasks, including cooking and preparing clothes. When Hearne set out again at the end of November, 1770, he had Mattonabee's seven wives, stalwart as grenadiers, in his company. They traveled slowly north-westward along the treeline, living off the land by hunting and fishing. Then they turned north across the barrens, gathering bands of Indians who were anxious to make war on the Eskimos. In July they encountered the Copper Indians and shortly discovered a summer encampment of salmon-fishing Eskimos, whom the Indian massacred brutally, while Hearne looked on in horror. Finally they reached the Arctic Sea, which was still frozen. Hearne uncovered no useful information about the Northwest Passage, and the "copper mine" proved to be a pile of rubble that, after a great deal of searching, yielded one large nugget of pure copper, weighing about four pounds, which he brought back and which now rests in the Natural History Museum in London.

On his homeward journey, Hearne discovered Great Slave Lake before he turned eastward and returned to Fort Prince of Wales on June 30, 1772, after an absense of almost nineteen months. Although he had not attained his major objectives, he had looked on the seas of the western Arctic. His geographical observations provided the foundation for effective charting of the northern regions of North America. He had accumulated a mass of fascinating information about Indian ways and attitudes. Finally, he had discovered new fur-bearing territories.

Yet when he returned to Fort Churchill in 1772 the direction of development had shifted. His next expedition, in 1774, was to the southwest, where the Company was opening its first post on the edge of the prairies, Cumberland House on the Saskatchewan River. An era of competition had begun that would eventually lead to the Pacific Ocean and to an empire vaster than even Charles II had dreamed of.

CHAPTER FIVE

The North Westers

After the Treaty of Utrecht French competition in the hinterland scarcely affected the Company's trade. The enterprise of the *coureurs de bois* was canceled out by the unimaginative royal bureaucracy in New France. All pelts from the interior had to pass through the *fermier,* a licensed middleman who operated the state monopoly in exporting furs and claimed a quarter of their value. The overpriced furs from New France were thus unable to compete in the general European market with those from Hudson's Bay, while the market in France itself was too small to provide an outlet for the whole trade.

When they began trading west of Lake Winnipeg, the *coureurs de bois* were also handicapped because their trade goods had to go by canoe over the complicated system of waterways and portages that linked Montreal to the prairies, while the Hudson's Bay Company readily brought theirs by ship to the southern end of the Bay. Canoes starting from Hudson's Bay could reach Lake Athabaska a month earlier than canoes starting from Montreal. Added time meant added cost, and since their market was so poor, the French had to be selective in the furs they bought. They bought only the lighter, easily transported pelts, allowing

the Indians to carry the heavier furs to Hudson's Bay, so
that the presence of a French post on a river leading to
York or Albany did not mean that the trade was entirely
cut off. After the end of French rule in New France, however, the trade route from Montreal did become a serious
rival to that through Hudson's Bay, and it was on the competition between these two routes that much of the frame-
work of modern Canada was to be built.

In 1759, when Quebec fell to the invading British army,
the French trading system collapsed, and the *coureurs de
bois* abandoned their posts on the Saskatchewan River and
north of Lake Superior. Some went to the Bay and offered
their services to the Company; most returned to Montreal,
where they and the voyageurs—the men who operated the
great trading canoes—found new employers.

Immediately after the Conquest, merchants from Britain
and New England descended on Quebec and Montreal to
fill up the trading vacuum left by the French. By right of
exploration the French had claimed the lands around the
Great Lakes, and the whole Mississippi valley down to New
Orleans—the original province of Louisiana. Thus, both to
the northwest and to the southwest, traders from New York
and New England found the way clear. The linchpin was
the fur trading post of Michilimackinac at the northern
entrance to the channel leading out of Lake Huron into
Lake Michigan. Throughout the British interlude, Michilimackinac remained an important center for the fur trade
in the southwest, but it also was the starting point for renewed competition with the Hudson's Bay Company to
the northwest. In 1761 at least two ventures set out for
Michilimackinac. In one of them a Frenchman was subsidized by a group of three British merchants; in the other a

Scottish trader, Alexander Henry the elder, set out himself and, after many harrowing adventures finally found his way to the rich fur territory of the Saskatchewan.

Here we should pause to look at the changed map of North America. By the Treaty of Paris, Canada—then principally the valley of the St. Lawrence, with its hinterland stretching to the Rockies—was ceded to Britain. Louisiana went to Spain, but Spanish rule was exercised effectively only along the actual course of the river up to St. Louis. The great plains of the West were an unclaimed wilderness inhabited by Indian hunters of the buffalo. West of the Rockies was virtually *terra incognita*. No white man had crossed that great range, and even the Pacific coast was little known. Russian fur traders were operating on the shores of Alaska, and the Spanish missions were moving into Upper California, but exploration of the coasts of Oregon and British Columbia still lay in the future. After the American War of Independence, the boundary between the United States and British North America was drawn slowly westward but not completed until the Oregon Boundary settlement of 1846. Immediately after the conquest of Canada a boundary was created between New France—now called Quebec—and the Indian country, where settlement was forbidden and trading required a license. This restriction did not last long. The enduring boundary was that defining Rupert's Land which kept competitors away from Hudson's Bay; it had been tacitly confirmed by a parliamentary commission in 1749. Outside Rupert's Land, a great western region of plains and mountains, soon to become known as the Northwest, was open to all comers. This became the great battleground between the Company and its rivals.

Essentially the rivals were a variable coalition of Montreal merchants and fur traders known eventually as the North West Company. Since the two companies ended their conflict by merging in 1821, the separate history of the North West Company is part of our story. In the years immediately after the fall of New France, the fur trade out of Montreal was handled rather haphazardly, by merchants who financed trading ventures into the Indian country. In the early days traders were usually French, but soon Scottish Highlanders showed themselves particularly adapted to the shifts and rigors of the trade. The first trade, as we have seen, was centered at Michilimackinac but in 1765 an expedition to the Northwest set out from Montreal. It was forced to turn back but in 1767 the independent trader James Finlay actually reached the Saskatchewan River. In 1772, a Company officer found many French and Scottish traders in the southern prairies, referring to them contemptuously as "pedlars," because they traded from canoes and temporary shacks. Among the "pedlars" were Alexander Henry, and a tough, New England ex-soldier, Peter Pond, who typified the ruthless energy of the new breed of traders out of Montreal. Pond in 1778 discovered the famous Methye Portage across the height of land from the Saskatchewan River to Lake Athabaska, the richest fur-bearing region of the northern forests, and his geographical hunches were to lead famous explorers like Alexander Mackenzie and Simon Fraser to greater discoveries. But Pond had another side to his character. He was involved in the deaths of at least two other fur traders; whether as the actual murderer is not known. But it is certain that he was a violent man who represented the lawless arrogance of the Montreal traders at its worst.

Year after year, as more men reached the Saskatchewan, trading became more fierce. Competitors offered higher prices for furs and dispensed rum freely to the Indians. When some of the traders tried to trick them, the Indians in their turn became violent. In 1776 no less than seven traders were ambushed and killed.

The Montreal traders realized it was high time for union. In 1776 a rather shadowy entity called the North West Company came into being, to be established formally in 1779 as a combination of nine different partnerships, holding between them sixteen shares. Originally a one-year arrangement, which was later renewed, the North West Company was really a series of loose agreements between changing groups of traders who every two or three years renegotiated the terms of their partnership. The essential aims were, first, to reduce competition between the Montreal interests and increase competition against the rival Hudson's Bay Company; second, to create a single organization for the buying and selling of furs; and third, to develop a reasonably safe system of transportation into the interior. Within the North West Company came together the merchants in Montreal who financed the expeditions to the interior, selling the furs brought back, and the actual Indian traders at the forts who were known as "wintering partners." This was an important difference from the Hudson's Bay Company; the officers of the North West Company were actual proprietors. The North Westers also had employees: the hundreds of voyageurs, and the clerks, really apprentice traders. But every important post was controlled by a man with a direct interest in the trade, and even the clerks could hope for eventual promotion to partnership.

Each year from 1776 to 1821 the fleet of North West

canoes—each able to carry four tons of trade goods—would set off from Montreal, the voyageurs singing their boat songs, and follow the Ottawa River, whence, by various portages, they would reach Georgian Bay and skirt the northern shores of Lake Huron to Sault Ste. Marie, crossing Lake Superior to Grande Portage on its northwestern shore, where a great depot had been built. Here the "pork eaters," as the men from Montreal were called, met the buckskin-clad "northmen" who came down with the wintering partners from the interior, bearing the fine winter furs. After conferences and riotous celebrations, the pork eaters would return with the furs to Montreal and the northmen would return to the hinterland before the rivers froze up. After Jay's Treaty in 1794, when Grande Portage came into American territory, the depot was moved eastward to Kamistiquia in Canadian teritory, and a great new establishment, Fort William, became the upcountry headquarters of the North West Company from 1803 onward.

The early years of the Company were not all smooth going. The Indians were still fitfully hostile, and in 1780 there were several attacks in the Saskatchewan River country. Their aggressiveness, which could have meant an early end to the Company's business, was tamed by a great small-pox epidemic along the Saskatchewan River, which decimated the Indians but also reduced trade.

At first the North West Company did not include all the fur traders. Peter Pond and his ilk remained apart. A reorganization in 1787 brought in most of the smaller traders, but the wintering partners became discontented with the dictatorial Simon McTavish, the Company's leading Montreal agent. Between McTavish and Alexander Mackenzie, the most energetic of the winterers, an enduring hatred developed, and a group of winterers broke away to found the XY Company, otherwise known as the New North West Company and sometimes as Mackenzie and Company; it operated from 1799 to 1804.

For a time the competition between the two companies was worse than that between the North Westers and the Hudson's Bay Company. The XY partners tried to set up posts wherever their rivals traded, and violence resulted, anticipating the struggle later with the Hudson's Bay Company. The rivalry lasted until McTavish died in 1804. Then the differences were talked out, and the XY partners absorbed into the North West Company. At this time they were employing 520 men in Indian country—clerks, interpreters, guides, and canoemen—as against 1,110 employed by the North Westers. When the union took place in 1804 the XY partners gained a quarter of the shares in the reorganized Company.

The history of the North Westers was marked by rapid expansion across the West. In 1786 Peter Pond founded Fort Resolution on Great Slave Lake; in 1795 Fort Augustus was built near the site of Edmonton; in 1799 Rocky Mountain House in the Yellowhead Pass; in 1804 Fort Simpson on the Mackenzie River. In 1805 the North Westers started trade west of the Great Divide by building Fort McLeod and Fort Liard in northern British Columbia; in 1807 they had built Fort Kootenay on the Columbia and were about to enter the Oregon Territory.

This expansion was preceded by a quarter century of explorations which delineated the map of western North America from the Arctic Ocean to the mouth of the Columbia. The names of three North Westers are particularly associated with these explorations: Alexander Mackenzie, Simon Fraser, and David Thompson.

Mackenzie was the first in time, and possibly also in importance. One of the few men Canadians regard as heroes, he was the first man to cross the Rockies to the Western Sea, establishing the claim on which Canada expanded to the Pacific.

Mackenzie based his first attempt to reach the Pacific on Pond's belief that a river flowing northwest out of Great Slave Lake eventually led to the Pacific. Mackenzie established a new post on Lake Athabaska, Fort Chippewyan, and, having put his cousin Roderick Mackenzie in charge there, he started his journey on June 3, 1789, with five canoemen, two Indian women, and an Indian guide called the English Chief.

They traveled from Lake Athabaska down the Slave River to the Great Slave Lake. After some days searching for an outlet in this immense lake, with its many islands and formidable storms, Mackenzie found the river of which Pond had told him. Little more than two weeks later, he reached a broad and marshy delta where the tide rose and fell gently, and on July 14, the day the Bastille fell in Paris, he was awakened by one of his canoemen, who had seen what he thought were "pieces of ice." Mackenzie immediately saw they were whales, and he says, "we embarked in pursuit of them. . . . It was a very fortunate circumstance that we failed in our attempt to overtake them, as a stroke from the tail of one of these enormous fish would have sawed the canoe to pieces." Mackenzie named the place Whale Island.

Mackenzie had not reached the Pacific. When he realized he was looking at the Arctic Sea, he felt that his effort had been wasted, and he named the great river he had followed the River of Disappointment. Later it was renamed the Mackenzie River.

He arrived back at Fort Chippewyan on September 12, having covered almost three hundred miles in just over a hundred days. Although failing to make contact with the Eskimos he had started friendly relations with some of the Slave, Dogrib, and Hare Indians along the river, and had found them an unusual group of peoples.

Because food was scarce, there were probably no more than three thousand Indians along the whole river, small bands of nomadic hunters and fishers, their light bark canoes and tailored clothing of skins decorated with "a style of peculiar skill and neatness." Though they had not yet acquired metal tools by trade, they possessed remarkably efficient tools made from stone and caribou antlers.

The territories of these tribes, rich in fur-bearing animals, were easily accessible to the traders of the North West Company; in the fifteen hundred miles from Fort Chippewyan to the Arctic Ocean there was only one major portage of twelve miles on the Slave River. Moreover, Mackenzie anticipated the mineral discoveries made there in later generations. At various places along the banks he observed perpetually burning outcrops of coal, and at one spot he found "pieces of *Petrolium*, which bears a resemblance to yellow wax, but is more friable." Today productive oil wells are in operation at this place.

But at the time, Mackenzie was disappointed with his failure to find an overland way to the Pacific where sea captains from England and Boston already were trading for the valuable skins of the sea otter and selling them for handsome profits in Macao. The Indians had told Macken-

zie there was another river beyond the mountains to the
west, and he decided to make a southerly attempt to break
through the Rockies to the Pacific. In the autumn of 1791
he went down to Montreal, where the Company's agents
received him with only lukewarm interest, and set sail for
England. By the next summer he was back, equipped with
instruments and new geographical knowledge. His cousin
Roderick, carrying out his orders, had built a post in the
foothills of the Rockies at the junction of the Peace and
Smoky rivers, 250 miles away from Fort Chippewyan. He
believed that the Peace would probably provide the easiest
way through the mountains, and in the third week of October he arrived at the new post as the first snows were
falling.

He wintered there, trying with little success to gather
information from the local Indians about the way over the
mountains. At times, during that long wait, he thought of
giving up, but with the return of spring his resolution re-
vived. On May 9 he set out up the Peace in a large canoe
which carried three thousand pounds of baggage, ammunition, and presents, and ten people; he was accompanied by
a Scottish clerk, Archibald Mackay, six French-Canadian
voyageurs, and two Indians to hunt and interpret. It was
an arduous journey. The canoe was too light for the heavy
spring floods, and as they moved into the mountains the
portages became hazardous. They had to make their way
along precipitous slopes and cut through forests thick with
deadfalls and thorny undergrowth. Their one stroke of luck
was to meet an old Indian who knew the country, and when
they reached the point where the Peace split into the Parsnip and the Finlay rivers, Mackenzie followed the Indian's
advice to take the Parsnip. This led him to a desolate land

on the watershed, where he met a band of Sekani Indians who told him of the "Stinking Lake," a moon's journey away. This he took to be the ocean and, following their directions, he eventually reached the Fraser River. At Alexandria, between present-day Prince George and Quesnel, he left the river and cut overland across a plateau and down through the coastal mountains until he came to the deep valley of the Bella Coola River, inhabited by Indians of the same name. The Bella Coola, who welcomed Mackenzie with great hospitality, were a people made prosperous by the vast salmon runs of the Pacific coast. They were also an artistic people and Mackenzie was the first European to record his admiration of the remarkable plastic art of the Coast Indians. From the Bella Coola villages Mackenzie and his party finally reached the sea at Dean Channel. His objective attained at last, he decided to leave a marker on the site. Taking some of the vermilion he had with him and mixing it with fish grease, he wrote on a rock bluff a proud and laconic statement: "Alexander Mackenzie, from Canada, by land, the twenty-second of July, one thousand seven hundred and ninety-three." He was the first man to come by land. But less than two months earlier, the coast had already been surveyed and annexed in the name of King George III by Captain George Vancouver in the *Discovery*.

For more than a decade after Mackenzie's journey, the country beyond the Rockies was left as a reserve to be exploited when the time seemed right. When Jefferson dispatched the Lewis and Clark Expedition to the Oregon coast in 1804, the threat of American competition moved the North Westers to act. In August, 1805, Simon Fraser, a Loyalist from Vermont, left Fort William with the in-

tention of establishing trade beyond the Rockies. Before
winter he had crossed the mountains and founded Fort
McLeod, on McLeod Lake, which lies beside the present
highway from Prince George to the Peace River. This trading post, whose vestiges remain, was the first permanent
white settlement between Spanish California and Russian
Alaska. Fraser founded two more posts in this area, and in
1807 he established Fort George at the junction of the
Fraser and the Nechako.

The territory beyond the mountains, which Fraser chris-
tened New Caledonia in honor of his Scottish ancestry,
corresponded roughly to the northern half of British Columbia. For some years it remained the center of the North
West Company's fur-trading activities beyond the Rockies.
An inclement land, remote from the Company's depots,
it could not be supplied easily, so that even pemmican—
dried buffalo meat pounded to a paste with suet—became
a luxury here. While the officers were reasonably provided
for, the men lived on a monotonous and unhealthy diet of
salmon, dried or fresh according to season, with an occasional roast dog as a special treat. A little agriculture was
practiced but basically the forts here—as elsewhere—remained outposts in a relatively unchanged Indian society.

Indeed, far from trying to change the Indians, on whose
life as hunters the early North Westers relied for furs, they
were inclined to adopt their customs. Most of them took
Indian women and only rarely felt an obligation to make
the marriage formal. Often the traders went further. Father
Morice, the missionary historian of British Columbia, states
that "instead of lifting the lower race up to the standard
of Christianized Europeans, the latter, in too many cases,
stooped to the level of the savages they had come to as

representatives of a wonderful civilization." Morice listed
as backslidings: "gambling, Indian fashion dancing, face-
painting, potlatching or heathen feasting . . . nay, in two
cases at least, even polygamy." The evidence in the fur
traders' own records substantiate this, but it must be remembered that the fur traders were well over two thousand
miles from civilization as they knew it, living the restless
lives of explorers continually on the move in unknown territory. In the end, the explorers' restless energy carried them
not only over much of British Columbia, but also over a
great part of Washington, Oregon, Idaho, and Montana,
and even across the Spanish border into California.

After establishing Fort George, Fraser decided to explore
the river that now bears his name. Like Mackenzie before
him, he thought it was the Columbia, whose estuary had
already been discovered by the American Captain Gray in
1792. The upper reaches of the river, passing through the
plateau land of the Shuswap Indians, were smooth traveling
by canoe, but in the great canyon of the Fraser, where the
river descends rapidly towards the Gulf of Georgia, they
were caught in the most formidable rapids they had ever
known. At times they had to cling to precarious ladders
which the Salish Indians had suspended on the sides of
sheer cliffs. Eventually Fraser reached the broad, smooth
stretch of the river below the canyon, and paddled down
the last hundred miles to a village of unfriendly Musqueam
Indians near its mouth. He took an observation there and
found that he was just north of the forty-ninth parallel,
whereas the Columbia, he knew, reached the sea at 46°20'.
He had come down a river which was not only impracticable
as a highway for the fur trade; it was also the wrong river.
But he had made an important geographical contribution;

today both the Canadian railways and the Trans-Canada Highway run eastward from Vancouver through the canyon he explored.

The exploration of the Columbia, from its source to the sea, was left to David Thompson, who, unlike most of the North Westers, was a Welshman. A professional surveyor who worked first for the Hudson's Bay Company, he moved to the North Westers in 1797 because he felt that their enterprising spirit offered a better opportunity for his geographical interests. Almost immediately he left on a journey through the southern prairies to the headwaters of the Missouri. The following year he went to the headwaters of the Mississippi. Afterwards most of his time was spent tracing the passes of the Rockies, with interruptions to trade furs and set up posts, like Fort Kootenay on the Columbia, which would establish a claim for the North West Company. Trouble with the Piegan Indians delayed his exploration of the southern reaches of the Columbia, and it was not until July 15, 1811, that his canoes reached the mouth of the river, having at last traced its whole course. He intended to establish a fort there for the Company, but the site was occupied by John Jacob Astor's Pacific Fur Company, which had established Fort Astoria.

This was a setback to the North Westers, but it was rectified shortly during the War of 1812 between England and the United States. At this time, the North West Company was reveling in prosperity. It controlled the trade over an area stretching from the Saguenay River east of Quebec to new posts far north on the Mackenzie and far west to the Oregon Territory itself—an area even greater than the Rupert's Land of the Hudson's Bay Company. One of its partners, Alexander Mackenzie, had been knighted for his explorations, while in Montreal the Company's representatives were commercially and socially powerful, dominating the city from the great mansions they built on the slopes of Mount Royal. They had far outstripped Hudson's Bay —two-thirds to one-third—in the amount of furs exported to England. When Thompson reached the mouth of the Columbia, many people in Canada and England assumed that the younger Company was bound to destroy the older one. Yet within ten years the North West Company was to lose its separate identity, while the Hudson's Bay Company would rule almost unchallenged over a territory almost as large as the United States today. The events leading to this dramatic change began to take shape that very summer while Thompson was hurrying down the Columbia in his abortive attempt to forestall John Jacob Astor's men.

CHAPTER SIX

Conflict and Union

On May 30, 1811, at the general court of the Hudson's Bay Company in the City of London, a time-honored principle was thrust aside. An article of faith among the *coureurs de bois* and the Scottish and English traders who followed them had been that land settlement was incompatible with the fur trade; where the settler appeared, it was held, Indians and the animals they trapped were driven out. Yet in the late spring of 1811, the Adventurers of the Hudson's Bay Company approved a grant of land along the Red River in the eastern prairies to a crusading Scottish nobleman.

Thomas Douglas, fifth earl of Selkirk, was a friend of William Wilberforce, the great abolitionist, and he had a burning desire to give practical witness to the Christian beliefs that inspired Wilberforce and his associates. For Selkirk, the compelling issue was not Negro slavery but the depopulation of large parts of his native land. As the Highland chiefs became landlords, they expelled their clansmen from the crofts tilled by their ancestors from time out of mind. Selkirk was one of the first British philanthropists to see the great open spaces of America and Australasia as obvious places to resettle his fellow countrymen, and the landless of England and Ireland as well.

In 1805, when he published his *Observations on the present state of the Highlands of Scotland with a view of the causes and probable consequences of emigration,* Selkirk was already experienced in the subject. Succeeding to his title in 1799 at the age of twenty-eight, he had resolved to devote all his resources as a Scottish peer in the House of Lords to the cause of the distressed peasantry of the British Isles. In 1802 he read an account of the Red River lands, and these well-watered plains seemed to offer a solution to the agrarian problem. However, his overtures to the Hudson's Bay Company were received coldly.

Selkirk put the idea away temporarily and began looking for other places to settle the dispossessed Highlanders who —he feared—would depart to the United States. He secured grants of land in Prince Edward Island and Upper Canada, the region north of the Great Lakes which eventually became Ontario. In August, 1803, he sailed with his first shiploads of crofters to Orwell Bay on Prince Edward Island, where he founded a successful settlement. The next year, after visiting Montreal and Quebec, and being entertained by the North Westers at their famous Beaver Club, he went on to supervise the erection of the first buildings at his Upper Canadian settlement, Baldoon on Lake St. Clair. At Baldoon there were difficulties over management, and the land proved to be swampy and malarial. In 1805 he learned that the settlement had been a failure.

The vast western prairies still haunted him with the dream of a great farming country. He felt that the Red River was the ideal place for settling the hardy Highlanders and Orkneymen. Since he could not persuade the Hudson's

Bay Company from without, he decided to influence it from within. First, he picked a somewhat incongruous ally, the North Wester Alexander Mackenzie, and in 1808 they began buying into the Company with the intention of gaining a controling share. How they could have come together is not known, for their aims seemed diametrically opposed. Selkirk wanted a strip of cultivation cutting across the highways of the fur trade; Mackenzie wanted access to the Bay so as to cut the costs of transport to the Saskatchewan and Athabaska regions and unite the fur trade from Rupert's Land to the Pacific. Mackenzie and Selkirk parted company in some anger, and the philanthropic lord then created a kind of family partnership with his brother-in-law Andrew Wedderburn (later Andrew Colville) and his wife's cousin John Halkett. Together they acquired £12,000 out of the £104,000 shares of the company and used this interest with strategic flair, to get virtual control of the Company's policy from about 1810 onwards.

At the meeting of the Company's general court in 1811 Selkirk at last fulfilled his heart's desire. He was granted 116,000 square miles of land, a fertile plain five times as large as Scotland, stretching south from the fifty-second parallel into the present states of Minnesota and North Dakota. The international boundary in this region was not to be settled for another seven years, and by then a great deal of dramatic history had been made in this gigantic concession.

The North Westers, who owned some of the Company's stock, were represented at the meeting by Mackenzie and Edward Ellice, but their fierce opposition tactics failed to budge the majority that Selkirk and Wedderburn had organized among the shareholders. The deed was signed on

June 12. Lord Selkirk's land was named Assiniboia. It was to be ruled by a governor with an appointed council, the first attempt at constitutional government in all the vast regions held by the Hudson's Bay Company.

The Red River colony was only one manifestation of the new aggressiveness that came into the Hudson's Bay Company when Selkirk and Wedderburn gained control. For almost four decades the Company had been uncomfortably aware of the threat posed by the enterprising ruthlessness of the North Westers. At the same time, no catastrophic reverses stopped the flow of dividends. During the long period from 1721 to 1808, only three years went without dividends, and this was because the French had destroyed Fort Churchill and Fort York in 1782. Even when dividends lapsed again from 1809 to 1814, it was not because of competition from the North Westers, but because the furs in London could not be sold in Europe during the war with France. Dividends had fluctuated between 10 and 4 per cent, but even 4 per cent was satisfactory in those days.

Yet even before Selkirk and Wedderburn, the Company had been forced to change. With aggressive traders working across Lake Winnipeg, up the Saskatchewan River, and into the headwaters of the Churchill, it was not enough to sit in the posts on the Bay waiting for the Indians to come down the rivers. For all their magnificent expeditions, men like Kelsey, Henday, and Hearne were really commercial travelers showing off the Company's wares. The Company had to trade where the furs were to be found. The revolutionary change took place when Samuel Hearne went to tap the trade of the Saskatchewan River and set up Cumberland House in 1774. During the next ten years the Company's expeditions radiated in every direction from the Bay: Brunswick House was founded on the Moose River, Gloucester House on the Albany, Hudson House on the Saskatchewan.

Canoe transport became a regular feature of trade on the Bay, but the Orkneymen who formed the majority of the Company's servants never became as adept as the French-Canadian voyageurs of the North West Company. For service on the larger rivers, particularly the Saskatchewan, the York boat was evolved. This was a flat-bottomed craft made of spruce, rowed by eight men with long oars, and directed by a steersman with a sweep and a bowman with a pole to push the boat's easily sloping prow away from rocks or deadheads. The York boat, which could carry up to five tons, was less easily damaged than the birchbark canoe. A flotilla of such craft, racing with sails spread across one of the great northern lakes, was a spectacular sight; but they were too heavy for use on the routes involving long portages. Their name, of course, was derived from Fort York, which soon became York Factory. With the founding of posts inland, York became a major depot where goods were unloaded from the ships that came into the Bay, warehoused, and sent to the posts in the western interior. This depot was the great advantage the Company had over the North Westers; it meant a month's less traveling time than the route from Fort William, and the resulting saving was one reason why the Company could pay dividends even at the height of the struggle with its rivals.

By the 1790s the Company's men were beginning to move beyond the confines of Rupert's Land into the wider sweeps of the Northwest. By 1795 William Tomison had established Fort Edmonton on the North Saskatchewan, almost within sight of the Rockies, and Peter Fidler had established Nottingham House on Lake Athabaska, in the heart of the special preserve of the North Westers. It quickly became a great race across the continent, with competing posts often established within sight of each other; only beyond the Rockies did the Hudson's Bay men fail to make a significant incursion by the time the two companies were united in 1821. At that time the Hudson's Bay posts numbered seventy-six, a vast increase on the seven or eight posts around the Bay only fifty years before, but still less than the ninety-seven posts of the North Westers.

One of the Company's most important innovations was the use of trained surveyors sent on regular journeys of exploration. Kelsey and Henday had been almost completely ignorant of surveying techniques, and Hearne's knowledge had been limited. The first of the professional surveyors was Philip Turnor. From 1778 until 1792 he traveled about Rupert's Land and finally into the wilder country to the Northwest, taking observations and charting the region. He was the first of the Company's men to reach Lake Athabaska, in 1791, and his presence there undoubtedly stimulated Alexander Mackenzie to hasten his journey to the Pacific. Apart from his own achievements, Turnor trained two much more celebrated North American geographers, Peter Fidler and David Thompson, who eventually became outstanding surveyors. Fidler was the Company's chief surveyor from 1796 until 1821. He went with Turnor to Athabaska and returned there later with his own party; he also surveyed the prairies. David Thompson remained with the Company until 1797, learning all of his craft while there. In his later work, and particularly in his definitive map of the western territories for the North West Company, he owed a great deal to the pioneer work of Hudson's Bay men like Turnor, Fidler, and Hearne.

In the early days, before the violence preceding amalgamation, the North Westers looked upon their competitors with more contempt than hostility, and in a way their contempt was justified, for the Company was unfit to wage a war of trade.

The loose partnership of the North Westers allowed great scope for independent initiative. Alexander Mackenzie was not acting under orders when he journeyed to the Arctic and the Pacific, and David Thompson was virtually his own master in the decade he spent exploring the Rockies and the Oregon Territory. The winterers, moreover, managed their posts and districts with a great deal of autonomy. This freedom of action of course was one of the consequences of the officers being partners in the trade.

Hudson's Bay men, being employees, had to work as well within a system that had become rigid with age. The committee attempted to supervise everything from London and this interfered with operations on the Bay. Even the freedom that distance might have given was negated by continued rivalry among the factors in charge of the major posts—Churchill, York, and Albany. The traders at the inland posts were hampered by the fixed Standards of Trade, so they could not compete easily with the North Westers, who would pay high prices in trade goods and dispense rum and tobacco to the Indians. Again, the economies imposed by London were reflected in the conditions of their employees and also in their meager style—an important consideration in trading with the Indians.

The North Westers traveled with flamboyant style, their

beaver hats ready to be donned on reaching an Indian village, their pipers' marches and reels resounding in the wilderness. The situation of Hudson's Bay men, on the other hand, is attested to by William Auld, the chief factor at Churchill, who spent the winter of 1808 at the Company's post on Reindeer Lake, halfway to Athabaska. In London the following year, he angrily described the post to the committee as "a Kraal" and "the most miserable hovel that imagination can conceive." The Indians, he warned, "must make shocking comparisons to our disadvantage."

Auld was also deeply perturbed by the armed might of the North Westers, and their unabashed use of it to impress the Indians and intimidate the Company's men, who since the last French raid on Albany in 1709, had led a comparatively peaceful existence. The North Westers had known violence from the beginning. After competition with the XY Company had resulted in a number of violent deaths, London became alarmed and passed the Canada Jurisdiction Act. Henceforth, criminal offenses committed in the Indian country were to be tried in the courts of Lower Canada. The act also provided for justices of the peace to serve in the Northwest: the first justices were all wintering partners of one or the other of the two companies. After the XY's absorption, they were, of course, all North Westers, a fact that played an important part in the later conflict between the North Westers and the Hudson's Bay Company.

At first, the North Westers' relations with the Hudson's Bay employees were not violent. It was rather a question of intimidation, bullying, and pressure. This was particularly so in Athabaska, which the North Westers regarded as their special domain, and in 1802 and 1803 Peter Fidler found it almost impossible to maintain his post there owing to such tactics; he left, after a winter's trading, with only 253 beaver pelts from the richest country in the North. Outside Athabaska, however, when officers of the two companies met, their relations before the crisis year of 1811 were at least formally cordial. Daniel Harmon, trading in the Assiniboine country in 1807, noted in his diary that "the greater part of the North West and Hudson's Bay people live on amicable terms; and when one can with propriety render a service to the other, it is done with cheerfulness." Rival traders may have been unwelcome in each other's territories, but so long as the Hudson's Bay men presented no real danger to the North Westers' control in the hinterland, the latter were prepared to observe the amenities.

At the same time, they kept continual pressure on the Company. When they failed, in 1784, to gain a monopoly over the Northwest similar to that which the Company held in Rupert's Land, they began actively to dispute the validity of the Company's charter. Alexander Mackenzie was not the only North Wester who saw the decisive advantage the Company had in routing its trade through York Factory. Duncan McGillivray had formulated a bold plan to break the Company's hold on the quick route to Athabaska and the Pacific. In 1803 McGillivray sent a ship, the *Beaver*, to compete in the Bay itself and dispatched an overland expedition to establish contact with it on James Bay. The *Beaver* anchored off Charlton Island and established a post there and later at the mouth of Moose River. This was trespassing, of course, but no court in England had jurisdiction, which meant that the only recourse was force, which the committee hesitated to use. Meanwhile, the North Westers used the *fait accompli* to press demands for a route through York Factory to posts in Athabaska and beyond.

In spite of their difficulties—the first real threat in ninety years—the committee stood firm, refusing to accept the terms offered for transit through the Bay. They also rejected an offer to buy them out completely. Their obstinacy paid off, for the Indians on the Bay refused to trade with the newcomers, and in 1807 the North Westers abandoned their posts at a loss.

By 1806, when the negotiations between the two companies were breaking off, the attitude of the Hudson's Bay Company was visibly hardening. But with the lapse of dividends beginning in 1808—even though the lapse was due to the Napoleonic wars in Europe rather than the North Westers in Canada—the shareholders understandably accepted an accommodation with the more accessible foe. There was another reason for their decision: a sharp increase in violence in certain regions when the traders of the two companies came together. In 1809 there was a serious clash in which the North West clerk Aeneas Macdonell came armed into a Hudson's Bay post at Eagle Lake and wounded two of the men there, before John Mowat shot him dead. The North Westers seized Mowat, kept him in irons over the winter on the warrant of one of their obliging justices of the peace, and sent him down to Montreal for trial on a charge of murder. He was convicted but pardoned.

Such conditions in North America explain at least in part why Selkirk and his relatives were able to gain control of the Company's affairs between 1809 and 1811. They represented a policy of enlightened self-interest: firmness mingled with philanthropy. While Wedderburn was an aggressive businessman, Selkirk was a crusader who was willing to use force to support his ideals. The two together formed a strong combination. Wedderburn was elected to the Hudson's Bay committee in 1809—just in time to challenge the policy of George Hyde Wollaston, the dominant member of that body. Wollaston was now proposing to recover from the wartime slump by selling timber cut on James Bay to the navy and by acting merely as an agency for independent fur traders who would operate from the Bay. Wedderburn regarded this as a counsel of defeat, a way to eventual bankruptcy, and declared the Company could recover only by retaining full and permanent control over the Bay.

Wedderburn found allies in William Auld, the chief factor of Fort Churchill, and in Colin Robertson, who was to play an active role in the events of the next decade. Robertson, a former clerk of the North West Company, had approached the rival company with an ambitious plan for seizing the trade of Athabaska by sending through the Montreal route an expedition manned by French-Canadian voyageurs who would be willing to put up a fight.

Wedderburn did not accept the plan at once but he recognized that Robertson would be extremely useful in the struggle ahead. His immediate aim was to reorganize the Company into two great departments, each with its governor: a southern department directed from Albany and a northern department from York Factory. Each department was to be divided into districts, supervised by chief factors, and thus an elaborate chain of control was established. At the same time, the officers in Rupert's Land were granted greater freedom of action; only the most important decisions affecting trade would now originate with the committee in London.

Selkirk's plan fitted into this reorganization. A settlement on the Red River would solidify the Adventurers' claim to the area. And it was no accident that the proposed site lay across the only routes into the Indian country open to the North Westers without going into American territory. Significantly, the Company, not Selkirk, made the first overtures. In February, 1811, he was asked to set forth his conditions for accepting a grant of land. The terms voted by the general court on May 30, 1811, were that Selkirk would receive 116,000 square miles of land for a token payment of ten shillings; in addition, he would supply the Company with two hundred servants a year. During the Napoleonic wars the difficulty of recruiting men in Britain had put the Hudson's Bay Company at a disadvantage in relation to the North Westers, who drew on an apparently inexhaustible pool of French voyageurs. If Selkirk's settlement provided a reservoir of labor it would be doubly useful.

Though a visionary, Selkirk realistically expected the North West Company to oppose his plan. His expectation materialized even before the first group of Irishmen and Highlanders sailed in July, 1811. Stornoway, the port of embarkation, turned out to be an unfortunate choice. It was the birthplace of Alexander Mackenzie, and the North Westers used their clan connections to persuade a quarter of the emigrants to desert, so that only seventy sailed with Miles Macdonnell, the Loyalist chosen as the first governor of the colony.

Macdonnell's reception at York Factory was almost as dispiriting as his departure from Stornoway, for the fur traders could not muster much cordiality for potential farmers. The settlers arrived too late to go inland before winter, and, since there was no room in the fort, they went up the Hayes River to establish winter quarters. It was a bleak, below-zero introduction to the land, and some chose to abandon Macdonnell and become laborers at York Factory. By the time Macdonnell set out for Red River after the breakup in 1812, only twenty-two men remained for the initial work of building houses for the first families of settlers, expected by the end of the year. Not until late August had he and his men gotten through the intricate network of rivers, lakes, and portages from York Factory to the mouth of the Red River on the southern end of Lake Winnipeg. On September 4 Macdonnell officially took possession of the Red River grant from William Hillier, a Company officer. Cannons were fired, the flag was raised, and the obligatory regale of rum provided to the Indians and *métis* (half-breeds) in attendance. All this was done in full view of the North Westers at Fort Gibraltar, but no hostility marred the ceremonies, which were attended by the new governor's cousin, Alexander Macdonnell, who was in charge of the North West fort.

At first the North Westers left Macdonnell to cope with the oncoming winter. He built his headquarters, Fort Douglas, nearby, intending it to be the nucleus of the settlement. But work had hardly started when eighty settlers from Scotland sailed up the Red River, women and children among them, with a piper playing from the lead canoe. After the first heady sense of arrival the settlers realized that the land was empty and freezeup due any day. Originally, Macdonnell had hoped to reach the Red River in 1811 and reap the first harvest of wheat when the second party arrived. But no field turned gold in those last sunny days before the first snows, and Macdonnell had to find food for the hundred people under his charge. He went down to Pembina, on the international boundary, and built a wintering post near the buffalo hunting ground where the Hudson's Bay men and the North Westers obtained pemmican.

Here a new element entered into the situation. The settlers had come to a country that was already inhabited. There were the local Indians, the Salteaux, who disliked the North Westers and were therefore friendly to the settlers. Over the border lived the fierce Sioux, who came north on buffalo hunting or horse-stealing expeditions. The Salteaux were no match for the Sioux, but the latter met more than their match in the *métis*, the half-breed sons of Cree mothers and French-Canadian voyageurs. The *métis* had already begun to establish little farmsteads along the Red River, but they were happiest hunting the bison on horseback, making daring runs into the heart of a stampeding herd and bringing the spoil home in Red River carts whose wooden wheels set up a squealing that could be heard for miles around. Through their Indian mothers the *métis* regarded themselves as heirs to the land, through their fathers as heirs to European civilization. They could be as fierce as Crees on the warpath; at the same time they were as proud of their identity as any racial minority in the age of nationalism then sweeping across Europe in the years after the French Revolution.

The *métis* were naturally antagonistic to the settlers— men who would spread over the prairies and pre-empt the land, driving the buffalo farther west. It was the old conflict between the settled man and the free roving nomad, between Isaac and Ishmael. For the first of three times in a century, the conflict was to result in a tragic confrontation.

At first, the winter of 1812–13, Miles Macdonnell was able to obtain meat and pemmican from the local buffalo hunters. But by the spring of 1813 the *métis* were beginning to refuse. And that year the grain crop failed. Macdonnell faced a second winter with inadequate supplies and more settlers due before freezeup. They were delayed, however, by an outbreak of typhoid on board their ship and did not arrive until June, 1814. By then only fifty-one of them were left—which made the food problem worse without providing the additional strength needed to counter the growing enmity which Macdonnell's actions over the winter had created.

In January, 1814, to maintain a supply of food until the land began to bear freely, Macdonnell issued a ban on the export of pemmican from the Red River and caused a cargo awaiting shipment to be seized. He based the ban on his authority as governor of Assiniboia, but legality was ineffective in the face of physical force. When the North West fur brigade from the Assiniboine reached the Red River in the spring, Macdonnell was forced to allow the pemmican to be taken out of the territory.

This was not enough for the North Westers. When the partners at Fort William heard of the incident, they saw it as part of a plan to cut off one of their main sources of food. There was a great deal of talk about offended honor, but the real issue was a hard-headed business one. The ban on pemmican was regarded as an act of commercial war and —carefully committing very little to paper—the partners let it be known that every means was to be used to destroy the settlement. Every means was used—including massacre and mutilation.

Meanwhile, Macdonnell had continued to act rashly for a man with little actual power. In the summer of 1814 he antagonized the *métis* further by forbidding the hunting

of buffalo on horseback. In October he issued another decree ordering the North Westers to leave the Selkirk territory within six months. The North Westers replied with
a campaign of violence masked in legality. One of their
partners, A. N. McLeod, a magistrate empowered by the
Canada Jurisdiction Act, issued a warrant against Macdonnell on a charge of stealing pemmican. It was an untenable
charge, since the act did not apply in Rupert's Land and,
in any case, Macdonnell, as governor, was the source of law
in Assiniboia. But the warrant was made effective by the
use of force.

When Macdonnell refused to submit, the North Westers
seized the settlement's two cannon, drove horses through
the young crops, burned barns, and fired into houses at night.
Macdonnell finally gave himself up. The settlers either went
back to Canada or retreated with their cattle to Lake Winnipeg. The *métis*, led by a half-breed clerk named Cuthbert
Grant, burned down their houses. Macdonnell was sent to
Montreal but was there set free: the aim had been merely to
disrupt the settlement.

Meanwhile Hudson's Bay was marshalling its forces.
Colin Robertson had finally persuaded Selkirk and Wedderburn to underwrite his plan of invading Athabaska with a
brigade of French Canadians. After sailing to Montreal, in
May of 1815 he led the first Hudson's Bay outfit ever to set
out from the St. Lawrence. With his customary flamboy-
ance—he was known as "Mr. Lofty"—he led his men dis-
dainfully up the North Westers' own route via the Ottawa
River and at Lake Winnipeg met the ousted settlers. Then
he led them back in triumph to the Red River, where he
seized Fort Gibraltar and rebuilt Fort Douglas. He was

happy to find that four Highlanders left in the Hudson's
Bay post up the river had saved the settlers' seed grain and
sown the fields, so that a crop was almost ready for reaping.

In the meantime, the committee in London had created
a governor-in-chief to rule over both of the great departments and also over Assiniboia. They appointed Robert
Semple, a grave, rather pompous, and entirely unimaginative gentleman of American birth. With a new party of
settlers, Semple arrived on the Red River from York Factory in November, 1815. For a while he and Robertson
worked well together, getting the settlement in order.
They also put up a good front against the North Westers,
whom they repaid in their own coin, arresting one of the
wintering partners, burning down Fort Gibraltar, and seizing the rival company's letters. In retaliation, Alexander
Macdonnell in the Assiniboine burned down the Company's post at Brandon House and seized its pemmican supplies at Qu'Appelle.

A state of semiwar developed as events moved towards
a catastrophe deliberately planned by the North Westers.
Lord Selkirk set off from England in the autumn of 1815
to play his own part in the drama. He had tried to persuade
the colonial secretary, Lord Bathurst, to send a small military escort along to ensure peace but Bathurst would do no
more than exhort both sides to stop warring. On reaching
Canada, Selkirk received news of the destruction of the settlement, and tried to persuade the governor of Lower Canada, Sir Gordon Drummond, to give him an escort. Drummond was under the influence of the North Westers and
he refused. Undiscouraged, Selkirk raised a private army
composed of Swiss and German mercenaries who had fought
in the War of 1812, giving the appearance of legality to their

presence by promising them grants of land. Armed also with a commission as justice of the peace, which Drummond could not refuse him, he set off in the late spring of 1816 by way of the Ottawa River and Lake Superior.

But Selkirk did not arrive in time to avert the catastrophe. By June, 1816, after a winter together, the flamboyant Robertson and the pompous Semple had tired of each other. When traveling weather returned, Robertson decided to resume his original plan of invading Athabaska in force. Accordingly, he left Assiniboia early in June. As soon as he left, the North Westers struck, and the result was the notorious massacre of Seven Oaks on June 19, the worst incident in all the wars of the fur trade. Governor Semple and nineteen settlers were slaughtered by the *métis*, led by the North West clerk, Cuthbert Grant.

Some Canadian historians have tried to minimize the North Westers' responsibility in this incident. Yet letters between the wintering partners leave no doubt that a massacre was planned and the time set for June. Two days before the massacre, the Salteaux Indians warned Semple that an attack was imminent. On June 19, Cuthbert Grant and seventy half-breeds, painted like Indians on the warpath, rode on the settlement. With thirty men Semple sallied out of Fort Douglas to meet them, obviously not expecting a fight, since he left his cannon behind and sent for them only when he realized that the *métis* were bent on trouble. The two parties met beside the river, and the mounted *métis* spread into an arc, outflanking the settlers on either side. One of the *métis* rode forward to meet Semple; there was an argument and Semple tried to seize the man's gun. A North Wester fired, and this was the signal for a *métis* volley. Some of the settlers were killed immediately. The wounded, including Semple, were slaughtered in cold blood and afterwards mutilated. Their bodies were left for the wolves until the Salteaux Indians buried them in compassion. Some of the settlers fled to Lake Winnipeg. Others were taken prisoner. Afterwards, the wintering partners arrived for a planned rendezvous and took over Fort Douglas, celebrating the occasion by firing the captured cannon and rewarding the killers.

Selkirk was at Sault Ste. Marie on his way west when he received the news. Immediately he diverted his expedition to Fort William, where he arrested the North Westers there, including the leading partner, William McGillivray. They were sent to Montreal under escort and charged with complicity in the massacre. In the trials that followed, only one North West employee was convicted of murder but even he was never hanged. And the North Westers, whose influence swayed the courts of Montreal, pursued Selkirk with counter warrants, entangling him in litigation until his early death of consumption in 1820.

In spite of these misfortunes, the worst was over. Miles Macdonnell, with some of Selkirk's mercenaries, captured Fort Douglas in midwinter and drove the North Westers from the Red River. Selkirk arrived the following June and spent the summer there planning roads and bridges, so that, in spite of early frosts and plagues of grasshoppers, the colony was able to survive and grow. The farmer had taken root in the prairies.

In the autumn Selkirk returned to his legal imbroglios. Outside Red River he left a heritage of bitterness throughout the northwest. The Athabaska region became the center of a conflict that continued almost without letup for the next three years. In some localities the North Westers tried to starve out the Hudson's Bay men by buying up all the food. Duels were fought between officers of the rival companies. Colin Robertson's first expedition to Athabaska, under the command of a subordinate, failed, but in 1819 he himself led 130 armed men to Lake Athabaska, and gained most of the Indian trade which the North Westers had monopolized. Then he was tricked into captivity and imprisoned for eight months in the North West fort on the lake, from which he ingeniously contrived to transmit orders to his own men by code. Finally he escaped, and the company's new governor-in-chief, a former ship's captain named William Williams, turned the tables on the North Westers by stationing an armed barge full of Swiss mercenaries below Grand Rapids on the Saskatchewan River and capturing the wintering partners and their furs as they came down from the interior. One of the partners escaped and died of starvation in the forest. Meanwhile Colin Robertson was captured a second time, escaped again, and fled to the United States where, at the end of 1820, he embarked for England.

At last the English government, conscious that if order were not reestablished its claims over the territory might be challenged, decided to intervene. In 1817 the prince regent issued a proclamation censuring both companies impartially for having "committed murders, riots, routs, and affrays," and he called on them to "desist from every hostile aggression or attack whatsoever." As events were to show, neither Company was impressed by this—or by a two-man commission sent out later that year. One of its members, John Fletcher, remained at Fort William in a drunken stupor, and the other, William Coltman, was a legalist unequipped to grasp the human complexities of the situation, much less the motives of Selkirk, that tragic near-genius. But later, when the scene of action shifted from the Northwest to London, the government did help bring a solution to the conflict.

Two of the hard-liners in the conflict, Selkirk and his former partner, Alexander Mackenzie, died in the same year of 1820. About the same time a rebellion sprang up inside the North West Company. Some of the wintering partners were disturbed by the growing violence of their own policy and worried about the financial instability of the Montreal partners. They were led by John McLoughlin, a fearless giant of a man. By coincidence, the ship that carried Colin Robertson to London at the end of 1820 also carried McLoughlin with a mandate from his supporters to find out whether the Hudson's Bay Company would consent to act as their agent. Meanwhile, William McGillivray, chief of the Montreal partners, had arrived in London, and Edward Ellice, Mackenzie's former associate, was carrying on his own negotiations for a peaceful solution.

On the surface, the North Westers seemed the stronger of the two companies, for they still controlled a much larger proportion of the trade. Yet the really important factors favored the English Company. It was a solid organization, with accumulated financial reserves. The North West Company remained a loose organization of partners and agents, and had no financial reserves whatever, since the profits were divided every year. The house of McTavish, McGillivray and Company, the Montreal agents of the North Westers, was actually approaching bankruptcy. The additional factor of dissension made union inevitable if the partners were to survive in the fur trade—and when union came it was substantially on terms drawn up by the Hudson's Bay Company.

When the union took place in 1821, the North West Company vanished from history in what was politely called "a deed of copartnership." The organization that emerged, with complete control over the fur trade from Montreal to the Pacific and the Arctic, was an expanded Hudson's Bay Company.

In one of the most important features of the agreement, the Hudson's Bay officers became wintering partners as the North Westers had been. This was confirmed by a deed poll signed by the Company and the fifty-three commissioned officers. For more than seventy years, until the early 1890s, the principle of copartnership between the Company and its chief factors and traders was maintained.

The British government watched carefully over the negotiations, which finally brought peace to the region. In 1821 Parliament passed an act for regulating the fur trade which implicitly confirmed the Company's rights over Rupert's Land. Explicitly the Crown was empowered to issue an exclusive license to trade in any part of British North America outside Upper and Lower Canada (part of present-day Ontario and Quebec).

When the license was granted, the Company's rule, commercial and political, extended over an area including the whole of the present prairie provinces of Canada, the Northwest and Yukon territories, the northern parts of Ontario and Quebec, and Labrador. By agreement in 1818 between the governments of Britain and the United States the vast area west of the Rockies between Russian Alaska and Mexican California was to be open to the subjects of both those countries. The British government assigned to the Company its rights in this region; since there were few Americans west of the Rockies in 1821, the Company thus had practical control over what is today British Columbia, the entire state of Washington, and large parts of Oregon, Idaho, and Montana. In all, counting Rupert's Land, the Hudson's Bay Company's dominion comprised more than three million square miles. It stood at the height of its power. But already the forces that would challenge and destroy that power were in being.

CHAPTER SEVEN

The Long Frontier

Despite appearances, by the time of its amalgamation in 1821, the Hudson's Bay Company was fast approaching obsolescence. Its trade could only be carried on effectively in regions inhabited by nomadic Indians—not in territory where people with democratic aspirations began arriving in large numbers. Nor could countries claiming even a degree of independence tolerate the presence in their territory of a vague and irresponsible government that received orders from a business corporation in the City of London. As the United States extended its control over the West and Canada grew from a few small colonies around the St. Lawrence to a dominion stretching from sea to sea, as farmers moved into Oregon into the 1840s, and miners into British Columbia in the 1850s, as the first settlers from Upper Canada reached the prairies of the Red River in the 1860s, the rule of the Hudson's Bay Company became a political anachronism. The Company had to change or to die. It chose to change.

We shall come later to the events in Oregon and the Canadian prairies which precipitated this change. Even before that time, however, the dominance of both the North

West and the Hudson's Bay companies was being challenged—not by settlers but by American fur traders and an
American republic slowly becoming aware of its full power.

Before Radisson and Groseilliers went to London in 1665
competition in the fur trade had been a two-way affair between the French and the English. When the Hudson's
Bay trade first started, the New Englanders had taken an
interest, particularly the Gillams, but after Benjamin Gillam's ignominious failure at the Bay in 1682, the Americans
left the northern trade to the English and concentrated on
competing with the French across the Appalachians and
south of the Great Lakes.

As we have seen, the conquest of Canada united the fur
trade south of Rupert's Land. The French gave way to
English, Scottish, and native American traders moving into
the region around the Great Lakes. By a royal proclamation
of 1763 the western posts of the former French domain
were set aside as a great Indian hunting reserve from which
settlers were excluded. It was an attempt to preserve the
Indian way of life, and so keep up the valuable trade in furs.

Traders from the Atlantic seaboard moved into the region
evacuated by the French, to Detroit, to Michilimackinac on
the narrows between Lakes Huron and Michigan, and to
various points on Lake Superior, from Sault Ste. Marie in
the east to Grande Portage and Duluth in the west. The
center of the trade shifted from New York to Montreal;
Grande Portage became the great entrepôt for trade to the
northwest, and Michilimackinac for trade to the southwest,
towards the Mississippi. In the interval between the conquest and the American Revolution, the trade remained
unified under the Montreal merchants. The War of Independence did not change this, nor did the treaty of 1783,

which recognized American independence. The British retained the forts on the Great Lakes, and under their protection the Montreal traders carried on business as usual in the country of the Ohio and the Mississippi and even in upper New York State.

After Jay's Treaty of 1794, which regulated commerce between the two countries, the British vacated the forts, which were in American territory as delimited by the original treaty. American garrisons and customs officers appeared, and restrictions were placed on the fur trade so that, though the traders were not actually forbidden to operate in American territory, they found it desirable to reroute their trade northwest through British territory, particularly after 1800, when an American customs officer arrived at Grande Portage. The old French route from Kamistiquia to Lake of the Woods was rediscovered, and by 1803 the whole of the Northwest trade had been transferred to Fort William. The trade from Montreal into the Southwest became a separate operation, and the Michilimackinac Company was formed for that purpose, linked with a trade agreement to the North West Company.

But the Montreal traders no longer monopolized the fur trade south of Rupert's Land. Americans were beginning to claim a share. On the Pacific coast, the first New England fur trading ship dropped anchor at Nootka in 1789, the year Mackenzie reached the Arctic, and in 1792 Robert Gray, a Boston captain, discovered the mouth of the Columbia. In the East, American competition with the Canadian fur traders was dominated by one man, John Jacob Astor, son of a German village butcher, who founded one of the richest families of America and whose descendants became British lords.

During the American War of Independence, the British

government prohibited the export of furs to New York. They had to be reshipped there from London. Jay's Treaty reestablished direct trade between Canada and the United States, and—since Canadian agriculture was still undeveloped—the principal commodity was furs. At first this seemed an advantage for the North West Company, which now had an outlet for their furs in New York, and they immediately came to an agreement with John Jacob Astor. But Astor had something else in mind. He used the profits from the fur trade with Montreal to expand his business, and soon he was buying directly from the traders in the former British posts on the Great Lakes, and so undermining the trade of the Michilimackinac Company.

Farther west, the international boundary was still unsurveyed at the time of Jay's Treaty, but the North West Company decided to discover which of its posts lay within American territory so that it could establish an all-British route to the Rockies. David Thompson's first task was to determine this boundary, which he did on a remarkable pioneering journey during the winter of 1797–98 along the Assiniboine to the headquarters of the Missouri. Thompson, unlike most North Westers a strict Christian, was profoundly shocked by the apparent looseness of morals among the Mandan Indians. He was relieved to find that the Mandan villages lay in American territory, so that the United States was faced with the task of bringing Christian morality to these happy pagans.

Astor built his trade with characteristic patience. Well into the first decade of the nineteenth century the fur trade on the Upper Mississippi and the Missouri was still mainly in the hands of the traders from Montreal. The great change began in 1803, when President Jefferson bought Louisiana from Napoleon for a mere $15,000,000. The United States obtained not only New Orleans, but also the whole country west of the river as far as the Rockies. Immediately after the American territorial government took over in St. Louis on March 10, 1804, Captain Meriwether Lewis and Lieutenant William Clark set out on an expedition to explore and show the flag, proceeding up the Missouri, crossing the Rockies, following the Clearwater and Snake rivers to the Columbia and eventually reaching the estuary on the Pacific.

Even before Lewis and Clark returned, news of the wealth of furs in the West had reached St. Louis, and small groups of independent American traders and trappers had gone up towards the dangerous Blackfoot country. But the field would not be left long to the independents. The larger traders banded together in the St. Louis Missouri Fur Company, and in the East John Jacob Astor obtained a charter from Jefferson in 1808 to establish the much more formidable American Fur Company.

Astor's company was the only American fur trading organization ever to compete on equal terms with either the North West Company or the Hudson's Bay Company, but it differed from both in its setup. It was a one-man business with a capital of a million dollars in the classic pattern of nineteenth-century American capitalist enterprises. Astor was the first tycoon in the fur trade.

By now the tide of settlement had driven the fur trade westward, and Astor planned to establish two lines of posts, one from St. Louis to the headwaters of the Mississippi, and the other up the Missouri to the Great Divide. He also hoped to take over the Michilimackinac Company so as to control the fur trade around the Great Lakes, and in 1809 he approached the North Westers with the suggestion of establishing a consortium to handle the fur trade on the Pacific coast, in which he offered them a one-third share.

The North Westers saw there was more to gain by resisting Astor. They rejected his offer and foiled his attempts to take over the Michilimackinac Company. Eventually, however, the Michilimackinac Company was merged into a new creation of Astor's, the South West Company, which he founded in 1811 with the Montreal partners of the North West Company. Both sides foresaw the oncoming War of 1812, and the South West Company was founded to protect the interests of American and Canadian traders. Cooperation between the two groups was so close that the British in Canada first heard of Madison's declaration of war through a courier message Astor sent to his North West associates. The South West Company survived until 1817, though its reason for being ended in 1816, when Congress excluded Canadians from the fur trade south of the border. Astor is said to have been responsible for the law, and it certainly cleared the field of his rivals, for from then on the North Westers ceased to trade in American territory east of the Rockies.

West of the Divide the only clear boundaries were the northern frontier of California at 42° and the southern frontier of Alaska at 54°40'. By the Nootka Sound Convention of 1790 the British had gained the right to trade on the coast wherever the Spanish were not actually established, and the Spaniards had made no effective assertion of their sovereignty. The North Westers were entrenched in New Caledonia, the northern part of the region, and by 1808 had penetrated as far south as the Fraser estuary. Below the Fraser, in the real Oregon Territory, the coast had been explored by the British captains, Cook and Vancouver, but there were strong American claims to discovery of the Columbia. Until 1810 when the North Westers established Fort Spokane, neither the British nor the Americans had established any fort in this great area.

Here on the Pacific coast Astor gained a temporary advantage. When his overtures were rejected by the Montreal partners of the North West Company in 1809, he induced five discontented clerks to join him in setting up the Pacific Fur Company. Astor proposed to send two parties to the coast, one by land and the other by sea, which in those days meant sailing round Cape Horn. The land party, led by a merchant inexperienced in the wilderness, took almost a year and a half to reach the mouth of the Columbia, and when it arrived in February, 1812, Fort Astoria had already been built.

Astor's ship, the *Tonquin*, had left New York on September, 1810, commanded by Captain Jonathan Thorn and bearing a party of fur traders led by Alexander McKay, Mackenzie's lieutenant on the great journey to the Pacific in 1793. Thorn, a former naval lieutenant, was a martinet, and there were continuous quarrels between him and McKay over spheres of authority. The ship reached the mouth of the Columbia in March, 1811. The fur traders picked a site and hastily built a fort. The North Wester Thompson came upon them in July, and was disdainful of their ineptitude at building and also at handling the Indians. Perhaps it was sour grapes; they had beaten him to the mouth of the Columbia.

From the start, misfortune stalked Astor's Pacific venture. In June, Thorn and McKay set off in the *Tonquin* to trade up the coast to Nootka. Thorn had no experience at all with Indians, and the peoples of Vancouver Island were noted for being prone to violence. Thorn made the mistake of allowing large numbers onto the ship and then quarreling with them. The Indians were cleared over the side only with difficulty, and McKay urged Thorn to sail away. But the captain refused and the next day allowed the Indians to return. Fighting broke out, and the Indians might have seized the ship if the powder magazine had not blown up during the tumult. All the white crew and a hundred Indians were killed, and the ship was totally destroyed. The greater part of the trade goods were lost. Only an Indian interpreter survived to bring the news down to Fort Astoria.

Meanwhile the traders at Astoria had established a trading network in the Oregon Territory. One party set up a post on the Willamette River to the south, and another, under David Stuart, blandly ignoring Thompson's protests that they were trespassing on British territory, followed him up river to Spokane House. Stuart established Fort Okanagan near the junction of the Okanagan River with the Columbia, and then, leaving Alexander Ross in charge, went on up the Okanagan Valley to the Thompson River, where in the summer of 1812 he established Fort Kamloops, well within what is now British Columbia. The Astorians thus succeeded where other Americans had failed—in establishing a fur trade beyond the Rockies.

Yet enterprise was offset by continued ill-luck. Even before he learned of the *Tonquin*'s destruction, Astor had sent out the *Beaver*, which reached Astoria in 1812 and then went up the coast to trade with the Indians and establish connection with the Russians in Alaska. The *Beaver* went on from Alaska to Hawaii and then to Canton, to trade furs. There her captain heard that war had broken out between Britain and the United States, and he decided to remain in China until hostilities came to an end. Meanwhile, Astor had sent off a third ship, the *Lark*, but it was wrecked off the Hawaiian Islands. Fort Astoria was thus left without any help or supplies, while its rivals—spurred on by the war news—were gathering around.

The North West partners in Montreal saw the war as an opportune excuse to expel the Pacific Fur Company from the Columbia. From London they dispatched a ship to seize Astoria but its progress was so slow that the wintering partner in charge, John Macdonald of Garth, grew impatient. At Juan Fernandez he persuaded Captain William Black, commander of the naval frigate *Raccoon*, to undertake the capture of the American fort. Anticipating a rich haul, Black agreed and the *Raccoon* arrived in November, 1813. But it was too late. When news of the war came over the mountains, Astor's men had retreated to the mouth of the Columbia, and the North Westers had gathered like ravens about them, with their brigades of armed French Canadians. Duncan McDougall, the commander of Astoria, decided resistance was useless, and in October he sold out the interests of the Pacific Fur Company. Captain Black found himself cheated of his booty but satisfied his pride by formally annexing the post and rechristening it Fort George in honor of His Britannic Majesty.

The Pacific Fur Company came to an end a few months later, but not Astor's resentment. This was one of his motives for supporting the expulsion of Canadian fur traders from American territory in 1816, and when the North Westers left he took over their trade and established his headquarters at St. Louis. He forced them out of the South

West Company, and in 1817 absorbed it into the American Fur Company. And immediately after hostilities ended in 1814 he persuaded the American government to demand the return of Astoria.

It was returned to American sovereignty, but only because of Captain Black's insistence on annexing the fort in the name of King George III. Had the fort been sold it would not have become the subject of an international dispute. But Black's little ceremony amounted to an act of war, and under the Treaty of Ghent all territory seized by force had to be returned. In 1818 the British government agreed that Fort George should be returned to the Americans pending a settlement of claims in the whole region.

The North Westers certainly had no intention of giving in easily, since this was the one region where they were able to reap the rich harvest of furs without competition from the Hudson's Bay Company. For five years following their takeover in 1813 they doubled their business in the Columbia valley and established new posts, including that at Nez Percé or Walla Walla. Late in September, 1818, the American naval sloop *Ontario* entered the mouth of the Columbia. The American government, anxious not to create an incident, had sent a civilian official, Judge Prevost, to take formal possession. But James Keith, the chief factor, refused to give up the fort and Judge Prevost merely nailed a board to a tree proclaiming the sovereignty of the United States. The impasse continued until the British naval vessel, *Blossom*, arrived with instructions from the colonial secretary to hand over the fort. The North Westers were infuriated, and some of the officers threatened to burn down the fort, which they had improved and enlarged. Keith finally yielded, but protested so lengthily against a ceremony that Judge Prevost contented himself with raising the American flag. He also agreed that the act was not to be taken as settling the fate of the post, and listened patiently while Keith argued that the fort still belonged to the North West Company by right of purchase.

In effect, the ceremony was a mere gesture. The North West Company remained at the Fort, which they still called Fort George, and on October 20, 1818, the American and British governments signed a convention opening the whole of the Oregon Territory to the citizens of both countries.

The result was, for a long time ahead, that the British fur traders remained dominant west of the Rockies. After the collapse of the Pacific Fur Company, Astor never again ventured beyond the Rockies, although Astoria kept a special place in his mind, and years later, in 1836, he commissioned Washington Irving to write its history. Other American fur traders crossed the mountains but were never able to make serious inroads into the North Westers' trading empire. Most Americans in those years were too concerned with affairs at home to be interested in distant Oregon; Washington was generally indifferent after the gesture of reclaiming Fort Astoria had been carried out. When the two British companies were amalgamated in 1821, and the flag of the Hudson's Bay Company flew over the seven forts of the Columbia region, the British future of the lands beyond the Rockies must have seemed assured. Yet within a quarter of a century that future was changed, not by military conquest, but by the westward movement of the American people.

CHAPTER EIGHT

The End of
the Oregon Trail

Nobody at the time described the entry of the North West Company into the Hudson's Bay Company as a surrender. There were too many proud men on both sides for the arrangement to be described in such terms. Indeed, William McGillivray made it known that he regarded the settlement as a triumph for the North Westers. There seemed to be some justification for this claim. Of the wintering partners entitled to a total of 40 per cent of the profits under the amalgamation, thirty-two out of fifty-three were former North Westers.

Yet any hope McGillivray and his associates may have held of eventually taking control were foiled by the superior organization of the older Company, and the wiser North Westers, like Edward Ellice, settled comfortably into the workings of the ancient committee, becoming loyal Hudson's Bay men.

Nor was there much chance of North Westers dominating the Company in Canada. A dry-witted member of the committee, Nicholas Garry, was sent out to supervise the unification of the two operations. At Fort William, and later at Norway House on Lake Winnipeg, Garry obstinately resisted Simon McGillivray's last-ditch attempt to apply the old bullying tactics of the North Westers. In the new dispensation even McGillivray's old associates balked at this, and he gained little support from the wintering partners. The former North Westers among them were content with their share of the profits under a more stable management, and the old Hudson's Bay officers were delighted to receive the same share of profits as their new colleagues. The result was that when Garry and Simon McGillivray met the factors in council at Norway House, McGillivray was opposed by a majority of the wintering partners. Against his plea that Montreal remain the center of trade to the Great Lakes and Athabaska, the trade was transferred to York Factory. Samuel Black, Peter Skene Ogden, Alexander Macdonnell, and Cuthbert Grant, whose propensity for violence was well-known, were excluded from the rights granted to other former North West officers, and when McGillivray demanded that Governor William Williams and Colin Robertson, who had repaid the North Westers in kind, be excluded too, this was rejected by Garry. In fact, Williams was given the governorship of the southern department, embracing the posts on James Bay and the Great Lakes, and was allowed to keep the nominal title of governor-in-chief. For the much larger and more important northern department, which included all the land west of Hudson's Bay, south of the Arctic Ocean and north of the American border, with the Columbia district as a semiautonomous administration in the far West, another Hudson's Bay man, George Simpson, was chosen. This appointment was probably the most fortunate of all.

Simpson was a relative newcomer to the fur trade. As small as Napoleon, and in his own way just as masterful, he was the illegitimate child of a Scottish clergyman's son who had been brought up by his father's relatives and was eventually employed in the London export-import house of Graham, Simpson, and Wedderburn. His uncle, Geddes Mackenzie Simpson, was one of the partners, and another was Andrew Wedderburn (now Andrew Colville), who was impressed by Simpson's work and initiative.

At the beginning of 1820, when the conflict between the two companies was at its height, and the North Westers were looking for revenge against Governor William Williams for arresting their partners at Grand Rapids, the committee decided to appoint a substitute for Williams in the event that he was absent from the territory. One can only wonder at Colville's insight in selecting Simpson, then only thirty-three and with no experience of life in the North American wilderness.

Simpson immediately accepted the assignment and set off in February for Norway House, where Williams had set up his headquarters. With a coolness that characterized all his action in North West, Simpson followed the North Westers' route and entered their stronghold at Fort William to deliver a letter from Lord Bathurst, the colonial secretary, enjoining both sides to keep the peace. He reached Norway House in October, to find that Williams had already foiled the plans to capture him, and that there was no longer any need for a substitute. But there was need for a resolute man in Athabaska and Williams sent Simpson on a special mission which had proved too difficult for three of the Company's most experienced traders.

Simpson set out like a veteran, leading a brigade of fifteen canoes up the Saskatchewan and reoccupying the Company's post, Fort Wedderburn.

The North Westers at first thought they could handle this novice even more readily than they had the formidable Colin Robertson. But lacking Robertson's impetuosity, Simpson bided his time until he provoked them into indiscretions and arrested their ringleader, Simon McGillivray. McGillivray escaped later, but then the North Westers had realized that Simpson was a new force in the conflict.

Simpson was building up the reputation that earned him the nickname of "The Little Emperor." Unlike any of his predecessors, he emerged from the Athabaska country in the spring of 1821 with a full cargo of furs and with enough standing to take a leading part in the council over which Garry presided a few months later at Norway House. There Simpson identified with the wintering partners and argued their case so eloquently that he soon assumed the position among them which had been held by the sick and absent John McLoughlin. When it came time to select a governor for the vital northern department, the nominee had to be acceptable to both the North Westers and the Hudson's Bay men. This eliminated many candidates, including Governor Williams, who tactfully expressed his preference for the southern department. The way was open for Simpson, and he was chosen almost unanimously.

Simpson looked after the Hudson's Bay Company's affairs until his death almost forty years later in 1860 at the age of seventy-three. After six years, Williams was recalled to England, and Simpson ruled over the southern department as well. He was, in fact, governor-in-chief, though he did not receive that actual title until 1839.

Simpson's immediate task was to carry out the reorganization that Garry and the council had mapped in 1821. He had to investigate conditions for himself, and became—in a way none of his predecessors had been—a great traveling governor. Today the visitor to one Hudson's Bay store in western Canada sees a dramatic mural over the main entrance. A large birch bark canoe sweeps over boiling rapids between the cubistic crags of Fraser Canyon; the swarthy voyageurs are paddling furiously. Impassive in these bituminous shadows and dangers sits an austere Scottish gentleman, wearing a beaver hat, a black frock coat, a white collar to his ears. It is Simpson in 1828, on his way beyond the Rockies.

That was the second of Simpson's great journeys, made almost entirely by canoe, to the lands beside the Pacific. During his early years as governor, Simpson let no year pass without some major trip of inspection. He traveled fast, usually in record time wherever he went, yet his appearance was rarely less than impeccable and his manner never less than grave and, when necessary, forbidding. He always approached a fort with flag flying and pipes playing and, watched by crowds of Indians, would pass through the gates to thunderous salutes from the ramparts.

However fast he traveled, Simpson never ceased making observations. He kept elaborate journals on the posts, the officers, the trade, the country, some of which were published after his death. Using this information, he introduced greater efficiency and economy into the service. New and faster routes were worked out. Posts were closed where North Westers and Hudson's Bay men had formerly competed. Redundant employees were pensioned off. With competition eliminated, the prices paid to the Indians were cut back to the Standard of Trade. Presents were curtailed.

In particular, the Company cut back on rum, partly because of criticism from evangelical Christians now on the committee in London.

Even after this retrenchment, economy remained a watchword of Simpson's regime, and necessarily so, for during the 1840s the Company was threatened by a change in fashion. In 1824 the silk hat had been invented. When it arrived in London from France, it was regarded as a shoddy substitute for the substantial beaver hat, but it was inexpensive, and by the 1840s the beaver had had become the headgear of the elderly and the conservative. For more than a decade the Company's business was in serious trouble. But with customary doggedness the committee and Simpson together kept the Company solvent until beaver became fashionable as a woman's fur. Henceforth, the furriers, not the feltmakers, were the principal market for the furs from Hudson Bay. During the crisis, the annual dividend, which had reached 25 per cent in 1838, did not slip below 10 per cent, and it never went below that figure to the end of Simpson's long tenure—attesting to the astuteness of his management.

This emphasis on economy did not mean there was any cutback in activity. On the contrary, in the Mackenzie and Yukon regions, and westward, in the Columbia district, Simpson's administration was a time of exploration and expansion. The aim was to open new areas of fur trading, so as to allow conservation in regions where the population of fur-bearing animals had been drastically reduced. Conservation had become an urgent problem. The introduction of steel traps, and the Indian custom of taking cubs and of hunting in the summer as well as the winter, had almost eliminated the fur-bearing animals in many regions. In the end Simpson introduced a system of quotas based on the fur-bearing capacities of the various districts. The only region where indiscriminate trapping was encouraged in Simpson's time was the Snake River valley in Idaho, and this was a deliberate policy—a "scorched earth" tactic to discourage American competition.

In most of the Company's territory, once Simpson had reorganized the forts and rationalized the trade routes, the trade went smoothly. The fur brigades came down each year to York Factory, and the Company's ships appeared just as regularly to unload their trade goods. East of the Rockies the canoes plied the narrower streams, York boats the lakes and the wider rivers. West of the Rockies, in New Caledonia, rivers like the Fraser were too dangerous for regular use, and the forts were served by brigades of pack horses which followed Indian routes across the mountains.

The two areas of special importance in Simpson's time were the Red River valley and the regions to the far west and northwest. Today the Canadian headquarters of the Company is in the prairie city of Winnipeg, which stands beside the Red River on the site of Selkirk's settlement. As early as 1815, Governor Semple had moved his headquarters down from the Bay to the Red River. It was an unfortunate choice then because of the conflict with the North Westers, and his successor, Williams, had retreated to Norway House and York Factory. But the Red River had its advantages, and until 1833 Simpson used it more frequently than Norway House or York Factory, his alternative headquarters.

After 1833, the Company's headquarters in North America was in Lachine, on the St. Lawrence east of Montreal, where Simpson lived in the same princely style as the North Westers had, particularly after being knighted by Queen Victoria in 1841. This return to Montreal was prompted by the Company's international responsibilities. Its relations with Americans in the Oregon Territory and with Russians on the borders of Alaska were matters of imperial concern, and at Lachine it was easier to communicate with Westminster, with Washington, and with the Canadian provinces, whose development towards responsible government was transforming them into a power of growing importance in the politics of the continent.

Yet to the end of his long tenure, Simpson remained aware of the special importance of the Red River valley. Its farmlands were a source of food for the fur trade. It was a good place for employees to be settled on plots of land when they retired. Even some of the wintering partners retired there with Indian or half-breed wives because—after twenty or thirty years in the Northwest—they could not readjust to life in Scotland or even Lower Canada. The settled valley was also a validation, as it were, of the Company's possession, particularly after 1836, when the Selkirk family abandoned the grant, and the colony reverted to the Company's control. As symbols of that control, two stone forts were built in the 1830s beside the Red River, Fort Garry on the former site of Fort Gibraltar, and Lower Fort Garry about twenty miles down river. It was to these forts, after Simpson's death in 1860, that the Company's administration returned, and Hudson's Bay House still stands—in the middle of busy Winnipeg—on a corner of the vanished fort's compound.

At the same time, neither Simpson nor the committee

in London could avoid the difficulties created by the agricultural settlement. The colony, a pious heritage from Lord Selkirk, was kept alive by the increasing importance of his brother-in-law Andrew Colville, who became deputy governor in 1839 and governor in 1852. Simpson spent much of his own time and the Company's money on ambitious ventures to aid the colonists, including a wood company and a tallow company—but all ended as costly failures. In the end the only way he would help the settlers was to buy their surplus flour, butter, and other products, and even then he had to placate the fur traders who ate dirty flour and rancid butter to keep the colony in existence.

It is hardly surprising that the Company displayed no enthusiasm for proposals made in Canada and England during the 1840s and 1850s for further settlements in its territory. When a committee of the British House of Commons held an enquiry into the Company in 1857, Simpson stated flatly, "I do not think that any part of the Hudson's Bay territories is well adapted for settlement; the crops are very uncertain." Simpson's stand was based not only on the fur trader's customary objection to colonizing the wilderness, but also on the many crop failures owing to early frosts; the quick maturing wheats now used on the prairies had not yet been developed. By 1857 there were eight thousand people on the Red River, but less than half of them could make a living by farming. The rest were hunters, trappers, and traders.

From the start, the need for some kind of political government had been recognized in the Red River colony, and in 1822, after the strife between the companies had come to an end, the council of Assiniboia was set up, consisting of three Hudson's Bay officers. The governor of Assiniboia normally presided over its meetings, but the Company's governor, whenever he happened to be on the Red River, took precedence, and in the early days Simpson interfered freely and autocratically in the administration of the colony.

By 1835 the transfer of the settlement from Selkirk's heirs had been arranged, and in February Simpson reformed the administration, so that the original council of three was expanded to nine, including the Roman Catholic Bishop Provencher and appointed representatives of the settlers, the independent merchants, and the *métis*. A Board of Works was set up, a customs receiver was appointed, the settlement divided into districts over which justices of the peace were appointed, and finally, in 1839, a court of law was established. The style of government was modeled on the British crown colonies of the period; there was no pretense of democracy, but an effort was made to represent various interests on the council.

Yet an inconsistency remained. Under the Company's original charter and the license of 1821, the Company was granted the exclusive right of trade. But in the early 1820s, a few *métis* on the Red River were trading with the Indians and selling furs across the border to the American Fur Company. At the same time independent merchants began to set up retail stores catering to the settlers. The Hudson's Bay Company opened a general store at Fort Garry in 1830, but otherwise did not interfere with ordinary retail trade. It stood firm, however, on its exclusive right to trade in furs. Simpson, realizing he could not effectively police the trade, introduced a plan to license settlers as fur traders provided they bought their outfits from the Company and sold it the furs they obtained. For the time being this eased the settlers' resentment of the Company's monopoly, but it also fostered a class of pedlars whose taste for profit grew. Trade over the border developed so much that in 1828 Simpson appointed Cuthbert Grant, now forgiven for his part in the Seven Oaks massacre, as warden of the plains, to police the border for the Company. Grant and the half-breeds kept the situation under control, while Simpson tacitly encouraged the licensed traders to work south of the frontier, until, in the 1830s, he made an agreement with the American Fur Company not to poach on each other's territories.

By the 1840s the situation had worsened, owing to the defiance of a number of determined traders led by Alexander McDermot and James Sinclair. And in 1843 Norman W. Kittson, an agent of the American Fur Company, arrived in Pembina with instructions to break the agreement with Simpson and capture the trade on the Red River. The illicit commerce started up again, more widely than ever, and in 1844 Alexander Christie, governor of Assiniboia, issued a proclamation threatening to seize the goods of independent traders who would not sign a declaration promising not to engage in illicit trading. It was a futile gesture, because of the merchant's determination and even more because settlement in Minnesota enabled the merchants to obtain goods from the United States without being dependent on the Company's transport system. Simpson managed to buy off McDermot and Sinclair, and the situation was stabilized for a couple of years by a detachment of soldiers which the British government had sent out. The presence of the soldiers intimidated those whose defiance might have been too open. But when the soldiers were replaced by a small detachment of Chelsea pensioners led by the ineffectual Major Caldwell, the illicit trade started up again stronger than before.

The settlers were angry over the British government's refusal to act on a petition, setting out their grievances against the Company's monopoly, which Sinclair had taken to London in 1847. Their anger was given shape by the leader of the *métis*, Jean-Louis Riel, nicknamed "the Irishman," whose son was to become the most famous rebel in Canadian history. When in 1849 Major Caldwell foolishly arrested Pierre Guillaume Sayer on a charge of illegal trading, Riel read a statement at the church door charging that the Company's charter was invalid and that free trade was therefore legal.

On the day of Sayer's trial, May 17, 1849, four hundred armed *métis* came riding in from the Red River settlements. The Chelsea pensioners were discreetly absent, and the Scottish half-breeds refused to act as special constables. Riel addressed the mob and urged them to free Sayer. James Sinclair stepped in and persuaded them to wait until he had pleaded the case as Sayer's counsel. Sayer was found guilty by the jury—the charges were never denied—but released without punishment. Although the verdict in effect confirmed the Company's monopoly, the *métis* interpreted it otherwise, and, shooting off their rifles, shouted, "Vive la liberté! Le commerce est libre!" And free, to all intents and purposes, trade was from then on. The Company turned its attention to the competitors over the border and soon put Kittson out of business with a brisk price war. After that, it let the independent traders rove through its territory, as a lion lets the jackals eat its leavings.

As we have seen, a whole series of ventures into unfamiliar territory marked the years immediately after Simpson's assumption of the governorship. In 1822 Fort Kilmaurs was established at Babine Lake in the north of New Caledonia, and the Bow River expedition explored the Rockies and their foothills. In 1824 Simpson called on those *enfants terribles* of the early days, Peter Skene Ogden and Samuel Black. They proved their mettle in two notable expeditions: Ogden's to establish trapping on the Snake River in Idaho, and Black's to explore the Finlay River north of the Peace. In 1825, pushing northward in the Mackenzie River region, Peter Warren Dease established Fort Franklin on Great Bear Lake. In 1827 Fort Langley (later the first capital of British Columbia) was established on the lower reaches of the Fraser. By 1830 the Company was pushing far north on the neglected eastern shore of Hudson's Bay, and Fort Chimo was built on Ungava Bay. In 1836 the first posts in Labrador were established at Hamilton Inlet.

This activity was carried out along traditional lines. On the Pacific coast, however, new elements appeared. Coastal ships began to play an important role, for the Company had to compete with independent American ship masters who sometimes sailed into the very estuary of the Columbia to trade with the Indians under the guns of Fort George. The first Company schooner in the Pacific, the *Broughton*, arrived in 1826, followed in 1827 by the *Cadboro* and in 1836 by the *Beaver*, the first steamboat in the region, which revolutionized transport. These ships established regular trade up the coast as far as the vicinity of modern Prince Rupert. In 1831 a post was established on the Nass River, and later Fort McLoughlin and Fort Taku were built on the far northern waters just south of the present Alaska border.

This expansion was not unopposed. Apart from the Americans, whom McLoughlin eventually eliminated in a series of price skirmishes, there were the Indians and the Russians. The Pacific coast tribes were an almost paranoiac folk, producing magnificent art in a ferocious contest for prestige and status. They were extremely volatile people, quick to take offense, and violent incidents were frequent in dealing with them. In 1828, for example, the Company organized a punitive expedition against the Clallam Indians on Puget Sound for the murder of a clerk, Alexander Mackenzie; twenty-nine Indians were killed and two villages destroyed before relatives of the murderers executed them to placate the Company. In 1829, when the Company's *William and Ann* was wrecked off the mouth of the Columbia, the Clatsop Indians murdered the captain and some of the crew. And in 1845 John McLoughlin's son was murdered by the Tlingit Indians at Fort Stikine in southern Alaska. Such incidents were unpredictable, and the Company's agents could do little to prevent them, except to remain alert and avoid provocations.

With the Russians competition was less unpredictable. At first, they tried to claim far more of the coast than they could possibly occupy, and in 1821 they issued a sweeping decree forbidding all non-Russian trading ships from proceeding north of 51°, which is slightly north of Vancouver Island. Neither the American traders nor the Hudson's Bay Company paid any attention, and in 1825 the Russian and British governments reached an agreement on the Alaska boundary which vaguely anticipated the present frontier.

One of the items left unsettled by the treaty was the right of navigation on the rivers that ran from British territory through the coastal mountains and down into the Pacific in the Alaskan panhandle. The headwaters of these rivers were British, their lower reaches Russian. McLoughlin, as the Company's Pacific representative, contended that his ships had a right to enter the estuary of the Stikine (in Russian territory) and proceed up the river to found a post on British territory.

This would divert a great deal of trade from the Russian posts on the Coast. When McLoughlin in 1834 sent Peter Skene Ogden to the Stikine River, Captain Zarembo with a fourteen-gun brig blocked his passage, while the Tlingit Indians threatened warfare because they feared that the Hudson's Bay Company would cut into their profits as middlemen between the Russians and the interior tribes. Eventually Odgen was forced to retire, and diplomatic exchanges followed, in which the Russian government accepted the British argument that British rights under the treaty had not been observed.

There followed a notable improvement in relations between the English and the Russians. Large corporations, unless locked in mortal combat, tend to make common cause against small competitors, who in this case were the Americans. Formerly American traders had paid for their presence in Alaskan waters by selling the Russians provisions. McLoughlin offered to provide the provisions at cheaper rates from the farms he was establishing on the Columbia, and in 1839 an agreement was reached by which the Company—in exchange for 2,000 sea otter skins a year —obtained the right to trade in the whole of the coastal strip of Alaska from Ketchikan up to Skagway. The Hudson's Bay men finally entered the Stikine without opposition, but, as young McLoughlin's murder showed, their occupation was not very peaceful.

The arrangement lasted until Alaska was purchased by the United States in 1867. It even continued through the Crimean War, when the two Companies agreed to maintain a state of nonbelligerence on the Pacific coast.

In Alaska the Company carried on trade in the old style, even making use of Indian middlemen as in the early days.

Southward, in Oregon, there was an immense diversification, largely due to John McLoughlin. It began with the establishment in 1825 of Fort Vancouver on the north bank of the Columbia. Simpson thought it likely that the south bank, where Fort George stood, would become American territory, but he still believed the British could hold the north bank. By then Fort George had a population of about three hundred officers, servants, and dependents, not counting the men in the upcountry forts, and McLoughlin decided to establish a farm for them at Fort Vancouver. The farm grew to three thousand acres, with great wheat fields, large herds of cattle, and flour mills. Other farms were established, and retired employees of the Company were incorporated into the farming venture, which was eventually formed into a distinct undertaking, the Puget's Sound Agricultural Company. Impressed by the magnificent forests along the coast, McLoughlin also went into the lumber business. Sawmills were set up, and this enabled the Company to spread its trade even farther than before—to the Hawaiian Islands and, in Mexican territory, to Yerba Buena, now part of San Francisco.

By this time, the Company's ascendancy in the Oregon Territory was waning. Americans were entering the territory, looking for furs and land. The traders came first. After the Pacific Fur Company failed, the Rocky Mountain Fur Company was established in 1822 by General William H. Ashley, and his officers, led by legendary mountain men like Jedediah Smith, got to the headwaters of the Snake River in the same year as Ogden led the Hudson's Bay parties into the same regions. The same mixture of conflict and comradeship prevailed as in the early days between the North Westers and the Hudson's Bay men. In the end the well-tried Company emerged triumphant. The American traders either succumbed to competition or were bought out.

But by the 1840s the fur traders were giving way to the farmers. They were preceded by the missionaries. In 1834 Jason Lee established a Methodist mission in the Willamette Valley, and two years later Dr. Marcus Whitman arrived with a Presbyterian group. Whitman crossed the South Pass from Wyoming in a wheeled vehicle, proving that it was possible for prairie schooners to get through the southern Rockies. These missionaries helped to stimulate interest with letters describing the agricultural virtues of the territory. In response to their urgings, the first party of real settlers came across the South Pass in 1839.

But political forces were also at work. In 1836 President Andrew Jackson sent William A. Slacum to investigate the situation in northern California and Oregon and report on the possibilities for a harbor on the Pacific. He was also to find out what the settlers on the Columbia thought on the question of American claims. Slacum's reports emphasized the power of the Hudson's Bay Company and declared that Oregon contained "the finest grazing country in the world."

Slacum created a new wave of political interest, which increased in 1839 when Jason Lee took back a petition from Americans on the Willamette, requesting the protection of American law. A number of congressmen, led by Senator Linn of Missouri, began agitating for military occupation of the Columbia and a territorial government for Oregon. But with the joint-occupancy agreement with Britain still in force, unilateral action would have brought danger of war, and it was some time before his efforts gained much popular support.

But the situation in Oregon was beginning to change rapidly. In a first official move to assert United States rights, in 1842 Elijah White was appointed Indian agent in Oregon and instructed to take with him as many immigrants as he could. He set out in May with 120 people. Half strayed to California, but those who remained strengthened the American group and provided a militant leaven, for after their arrival the first steps towards local government were taken. On May 2, 1843, the settlers in the Willamette Valley narrowly passed a resolution to create a provisional government.

The provisional government rested on insecure foundations, for the American population did not equal the number of British subjects attached to the Hudson's Bay Company. Any other chief factor than John McLoughlin would have resisted the settlers. But McLoughlin cooperated with them, using the resources of his posts to help nine hundred arrivals in the immigration of 1843. In this, he helped decide the Oregon issue for the Americans, since it was this group that finally swung the population balance.

McLoughlin was censured by Governor Simpson for helping the immigrants, and it seems likely that his loyalty to the Company had grown thin because he resented Simpson's autocratic ways. But it is hard to see what else he could have done. The few fur traders and their men could not have stemmed the flood of people: in 1844 another fourteen hundred came and in 1845 three thousand, raising the American population to almost six thousand. The British traders, and the additional *métis* settlers Simpson had sent out, were now many times outnumbered.

During these years, the political issue reached its most

dangerous point. This is not the place to tell the story of the American political campaigns to annex the whole of the Pacific coast from Mexico to Alaska, including what is now British Columbia. It is enough to say that a compromise was reached eventually between the American and British governments recognizing the forty-ninth parallel as the international boundary from the Rockies to the sea, with the proviso that all of Vancouver Island should remain British and that the Hudson's Bay Company should retain navigation rights on the Columbia. This wiped out the Company's exclusive rights in the great area which is now Washington, Oregon, and Idaho.

Simpson and his subordinates had foreseen this ending and were already prepared. As early as 1837 McLoughlin sent the *Beaver to* Vancouver Island to find a site for a large post, suitable for farming, with a good harbor and timber. A harbor surrounded by natural parkland was discovered, and six years later Chief Factor James Douglas went out to establish the new post. In 1843 construction of the fort began. It was called Victoria, after the young queen, and eventually it replaced Fort Vancouver as the Company's headquarters on the Pacific coast. In 1860 the Company closed its dwindling trade in Oregon, giving up its land and forts, and in 1869 the United States granted $650,000 in final payment for the rights the Company had lost in 1846.

CHAPTER NINE

An Empire Lost

Today, in the 1970s, the Hudson's Bay Company is divided into two great branches: the department stores in the prairie cities and on the Pacific coast, and the northern stores scattered across the Arctic and the sub-Arctic, where the Company still enjoys a near monopoly in the fur trade. In 1821 very few of these northern communities were within the Company's sphere of activity; they were north of the tree line, where beaver did not live. With the decline of the beaver hat in the 1840s, a change in the trade took place which coincided happily with the Company's forced retreat from the Columbia.

Once furs were sought, rather than pelts for felting, the Mackenzie River gained a new importance in the Company's plans. On the Barren Lands marten and fox were abundant, and in the marshy delta through which the river empties into the Arctic Ocean there were many muskrats. The forts along the Mackenzie and on connecting lakes were expanded. Eventually eleven posts in the region were trading with Eskimos as well as Indians, and by the middle of the century the profit from this trade amounted to more than thirty thousand pounds a year. The Company's men also pushed into the Yukon region, planting posts on the Pelly River, and in 1847 founding Fort Yukon. It lay within Russian territory, but the Company traded unmolested there until after Alaska became American in 1867.

In the Mackenzie Valley the peculiar conditions needed for the fur trade were preserved by distance and climate. The summers were too short and the markets too distant for either commercial farming or cattle breeding. At the more southerly posts like Fort Simpson and Fort Resolution, the traders grew considerable quantities of crops like potatoes, turnips, and barley. Fisheries were established, particularly on Great Slave Lake, whose whitefish is still famous, and the Indians supplied large quantities of rabbits, dried caribou meat, and pemmican, for which they used moose meat, since the buffalo did not range so far north. But there was nothing to attract settlers and the old simple relationship between trapper and trader was preserved. Mining did not interfere until the Klondike gold rush of 1898, and there was no serious competition from the independent fur traders who edged into the territory until the 1880s.

The Company was establishing itself in far northern regions which had aroused hardly any interest in the days when the beaver was king. For the first time the Eskimos entered into the Company's operations as seal and whale hunters and trappers of the Arctic fox. And for the first time in many years Samuel Hearne's account of his great journey to the Coppermine River was reexamined, as new explorations into northern regions were subsidized by the committee.

The decision to undertake these expeditions stemmed

from several motives. There was, first, the desire to find new trade. It was also important to reassert the Company's claims to the northern regions by exploration where actual occupation was impossible. Most important perhaps, was the need to counteract English exploration of the North, stimulated by a new interest in the Northwest Passage following on Sir John Franklin's first expedition. Apart from genuine scientific enthusiasm, the Company's claims would have been weakened if it remained idle while Her Majesty's Navy was actively exploring the far North.

Accordingly, when Franklin set out on his second Arctic expedition, Chief Factor Peter Warren Dease was deputed to accompany him. It was on this expedition that Dease founded Fort Franklin on Great Bear Lake.

Eleven years later, in 1836, the Company decided to enter Arctic exploration on its own initiative and offered the British government to carry on Franklin's work. It was anxious to forestall the Russians and also to frustrate its enemies in England at a critical time when its license to trade would be coming up for renewal. It succeeded in both aims. The Russians had not even started their expedition before the Company's had shown dramatic results, while the license was gratefully renewed by the British government in 1838, four years ahead of time.

The Company's expedition was headed by Dease and Thomas Simpson, a young cousin of the governor. Dease was by now an experienced northern traveler. Simpson was a difficult young man, subject to deep depressions, but extremely energetic and resourceful. While Dease at Fort Chippewyan made the preparations for the expedition, Simpson spent the summer and autumn of 1836 at Red

River, perfecting his knowledge of surveying and astronomy. At the end of November, they set off by dog team from Fort Garry to Lake Athabaska, covering the 1,377 miles in sixty-two days. In June, 1837, the two explorers left Fort Chippewyan, descending the Slave and Mackenzie rivers to the Arctic and then exploring the coast westward to Point Barrow in Alaska. This closed the gap between Franklin's charts of the western Arctic and the existing charts of the Pacific. The explorers returned up the Mackenzie and crossed to Great Bear Lake, where they set up a post called Fort Confidence and wintered there. Next year, at breakup, they traveled across country from Great Bear Lake to the Coppermine River and sailed down its rather tempestuous course to the sea. There they explored the coastline beyond Franklin's eastermost point and reached Cape Beaufort before turning back to spend another winter at Fort Confidence. Finally, in 1839, they returned to the Coppermine, and in the most remarkable part of their expedition, explored Queen Maud Gulf and parts of Victoria Island and King William Island. They got within ninety miles of the Magnetic Pole and came very near to solving the secret of the Northwest Passage. When they finished, the whole western Arctic coastline had been charted from Boothia Peninsula to the Pacific. Had he lived, Simpson might indeed have completed the task of tracing the Northwest Passage. "I feel an irresistible presentiment that I am destined to bear the Honourable Company's flag fairly through and out of the Polar Sea," he wrote after returning to Fort Garry. But that same year he died mysteriously while passing through the Sioux country with a group of half-breeds; the fact that he detested the *métis* and was hated by them in turn has always left the suspicion that he did not commit suicide, as they asserted, but was murdered by them.

Dease and Simpson had demonstrated, as Hearne did long before, that the best results were obtained by traveling unencumbered and living off the land as much as possible. Tragically, official explorers like Franklin disdained their example. Franklin's last expedition ended in death for him and his men in 1847. The expedition carried too much elaborate equipment, and there were too many men, untrained in the art of survival in the North.

The expeditions sent out to search for Franklin after his disappearance finally established the existence of a Northwest Passage, though the old dream of a ready route to China was shattered, since the passage was choked with ice most of the time. (It was not until 1906 that Roald Amundsen actually sailed a ship through the passage, and not until 1944 that Henry Larsen of the Royal Canadian Mounted Police showed that it was sometimes possible to make the trip in a single season.) The commercial hopes for the Northwest Passage thus proved illusory, but the explorers who determined this, as a side result of their search for Franklin, also helped complete the chart of the Arctic region.

The most notable of the explorers was a physician, Dr. James Rae. In 1854 he returned from the last of five Arctic trips with a report that he had spoken with Eskimo witnesses of Franklin's death on King William Island. Rae was a prime example of adaptation to the rigors of life in the North. Under Eskimo tutelage, he became so hardy an explorer that he was reputed to be able to cover a hundred miles in two days on snowshoes. All his expeditions were carried out by small boat and sleigh, and food obtained almost entirely by hunting. Rae was the last of the great explorers in the fur trade, and he may well have been the greatest, for none of the others showed so completely how,

with the starkest means, a man who knows the land can
survive and triumph even in the most trying of environ-
ments.

In the North at mid-century the Company was free to
continue operations according to its traditional methods.
But southward, along the border established by the Oregon
boundary agreement, it still faced the problem of new
colonization that had already robbed it of the rich province
on the Columbia. Even in the vast territories remaining
to it north of the forty-ninth parallel, its interests could be
endangered by an unregulated influx of settlers. The solution to this, it seemed to the committee in London, was to
secure *de jure* government over the area. Accordingly, in
September, 1846, the governor in England, Sir John Henry
Pelly, addressed a note to the colonial secretary, Earl Grey,
sounding out the British government's intentions. The
following March, in another letter, Pelly went further, offering the Company's services as an agency for colonizing and
governing the area, adding the Company's readiness to receive a grant of "all territories belonging to the Crown,
which are situated north and west of Rupert's Land."

This bid, for what in effect was a monopoly of colonization over an area almost equal to the present United States,
was more than the most sympathetic English politician
could seriously consider. The Company then reduced its
demands to the territory west of the Rockies. The eventual
concession was limited to Vancouver Island, although with
complete control of the island and exclusive trading privileges as far as the boundaries of Upper Canada, the Company occupied an apparently unassailable position in the
British territories beyond the Rockies.

The only limiting factor was the appointment of the governor of Vancouver Island. The Company had pressed for its chief factor, James Douglas, but the colonial secretary appointed an independent, Richard Blanshard, a former West Indian official. Blanshard was given a systematically bad time by the Hudson's Bay officials. They overcharged him for his supplies, delayed providing housing or office accommodation, gave him no assistance at all in his public functions, and deliberately withheld important information. Blanshard found his task impossible and resigned in 1851, to the regret of the few independent colonists who had arrived by this time. When the Colonial Office gave in and appointed James Douglas the new governor, the colonists protested in a memorandum pointing out that Douglas could not govern impartially and warning of strife with the Company.

The settlers' protest was unavailing but prophetic. Their running feud with Douglas continued throughout his administration, and the governor's actions showed a perpetual desire to safeguard the Company's interests. As judge of the Supreme Court he appointed a brother-in-law who had no legal experience. When Henry Labouchere, then colonial secretary, instructed him in 1856 to call a legislative assembly, Douglas agreed reluctantly, but restricted the property qualifications for the election and packed the assembly with Company employees. When the body finally met, he insisted on standing—as far as financial matters were concerned—on the letter of the Company's grant. All revenues from land sales and coal and timber royalties were to be used by the Company as it saw fit; only the fees from licensed taverns were within the province of the legislators! At the same time, in his other office as chief factor, Douglas obliged the settlers to sell their produce to the Company at buyer's prices, while charging them four times the London cost for anything they bought. In view of this, it is not surprising that the parliamentary select committee which met in 1857 to review the Company's position decided that its interests on Vancouver Island interfered with the development of healthy representative institutions. The committee recommended that the Company's colonizing rights be revoked.

This left the Company with the Indian trading monopoly and with virtually complete control over New Caledonia— the mainland of modern British Columbia. By 1858, however, another irruption from the outside world hastened the end of Company rule over this territory. In 1855 gold was discovered on the Columbia, and a little later on the Thompson. At first mining was small-scale but by 1857, when a Company ship reached San Francisco with a modest amount of gold dust for assay, the news was out. That year the first prospectors appeared from the worked-out minefields of California, and the following year there was a stampede. During that season nearly thirty thousand miners sailed up the Fraser in any vessel that seemed likely to stay afloat. These newcomers, all breathing democratic fire, altered the whole situation, and Douglas realized he must act quickly to preserve the Company's monopoly. As governor of Vancouver Island he had no political authority elsewhere, but, adding for the occasion the words "And Dependencies" to his title "Governor of Vancouver Island," he proclaimed that no boat could travel on the Lower Fraser without a Company license, and that every miner should pay it a head tax of two dollars.

These efforts to shore up the disintegrating fur empire

were unsuccessful. On July 16, 1858, Sir Edward Bulwer-Lytton, the colonial secretary, overruled Douglas. It was the death knell for the Company's territorial power in New Caledonia, and the warning bell for its power elsewhere. The miners continued to arrive in the thousands—forty-niners from California, overlanders from eastern Canada, Europeans of every race, and a leavening of Chinese, who would rework the tailings which other miners had left. The situation demanded a new form of government, and on September 2, 1858, the crown colony of British Columbia was founded and the Company's license to exclusive trade west of the Rockies was revoked. Douglas was made governor of the new colony, and remained governor of Vancouver Island, but only on condition that he severed his connection with the Company. In 1862 the crown took back all rights over Vancouver Island. In the end on the Pacific coast the Company was reduced to the status of another trading company whose only advantage over its competitors lay in its long experience.

The events in British Columbia portended the disintegration of the Company's monopoly throughout the rest of British North America. As early as 1857, a parliamentary committee had indicated the direction of future events when, with the Red River and Saskatchewan valleys in mind, its members concluded that Canada—meaning the united province of Upper and Lower Canada (Ontario and Quebec)—was justified in wishing to annex neighboring territory for purposes of settlement. At the end of the eighteenth century, when Loyalists began immigrating to Upper Canada, there was land enough to spare in the great forests which stretched to the north of Lakes Erie and Ontario. But by the 1850s, after the great influx from the British Isles, the forests had fallen and the good land been taken up. Upper Canada began to look towards the great empty prairies on the other side of the wilderness of rocks and muskeg—the vast and ancient geological formation known as the pre-Cambrian Shield—which lies to the north of Lake Superior.

By the late 1850s, Upper Canadian politicians were talking of taking over the prairie region. But these were years of internal political problems. The English of Upper Canada and the French of Lower Canada were locked into a single province despite their differing cultures; the four tiny colonies of the Maritimes—Nova Scotia, New Brunswick, Prince Edward Island, and Newfoundland—were unsure of their future. Not until the early 1860s was the solution of confederation widely accepted, and not until 1867 did Canada emerge as a union of the four provinces of Ontario, Quebec, Nova Scotia, and New Brunswick, with ambitions to create a nation stretching from the Atlantic to the Pacific. The main obstacle to that ambition was the Hudson's Bay Company with its charter rights in Rupert's Land and its trading monopoly over the prairies and the north as far as the Rocky Mountains.

But the Company had anticipated changes that confederation would bring. It had already undergone deep internal changes, owing partly to the deaths of some of its leading figures in the past. Andrew Colville died in 1856 and Sir George Simpson in 1860. In the far West, the dismantling of the Company's great estate had begun. In 1861 it began to sell its lands in Victoria; the following year it disposed of its coal mines in Nanaimo. A new means of wealth was uncovered when empty land found men who needed it.

This was not lost on certain financiers of the City of

London who, at the beginning of the 1860s, looked on the Company with a new interest. When their first approach was made to Governor Henry Hulse Berens, twentieth in succession from Rupert of the Rhine, it came from the most aristocratic levels, as befitted so venerable a Company. The duke of Newcastle forwarded to the governor a letter from a number of interested gentlemen, headed by Thomas Baring, M.P., of the famous banking family, and Edward Watkin, who had been deeply involved in Canadian railway ventures. They expressed their interest in forming a company to open a route "for Passenger Traffic and Telegraphic Communication" across the continent. They also proposed to build a wagon road across the prairies to British Columbia.

This was but a discreet way of introducing the real aim of Baring, Watkin, and their associates, which was to take over the Hudson's Bay Company. A year of negotiations followed, and the committee bargained first reluctantly and then toughly. In the end stock was bought for a million and a half pounds, the original proprietors selling their shares to a special syndicate, the International Finance Society. The proprietors were satisfied, for they received £300 each for shares which shortly before had stood at less than £200.

The wintering partners, however, were not even consulted and left to make their arrangements with the new proprietors. This was regarded as betrayal in the trading forts and factories, and the bad feeling was never quite removed. The winterers resented the appointment of Curtis Miranda Lampson, a former American fur trader and competitor, as deputy governor of the reorganized Company, under Governor Sir Edmund Head, former governor general of

Canada. They were also afraid that the fur trade would be neglected for real estate transactions. And they suspected that their share of the profits was endangered—not without cause, for the new committee contemplated terminating the deed poll and turning the Company's officers into salaried employees. A mass resignation became a possibility, and the committee diplomatically retreated.

The new committee lost little time in attempting to realize money on its vast territory (896,000,000 acres according to the prospectus). It offered to sell its rights over the southern portion of Rupert's Land to the British government for the sum of one million pounds. The colonial secretary countered with an offer of a quarter million, paid as the land was sold to incoming settlers. The committee accepted the suggestion that payment should be related to land sales but stood firm on its original figure.

By then Canada had intervened, criticizing the validity of the Company's charter and maintaining that it alone had the right to acquire the Northwest. The Colonial Office agreed, and from here on, until the Company finally surrendered its rights in 1869, three-way negotiations were under way between Canada, the Colonial Office, and the Company.

At least one powerful outside interest tried to enter negotiations—the United States Senate, which in 1868 passed resolutions offering $6,000,000 to the Hudson's Bay Company for its rights in Rupert's Land and the Northwest. This was too late and too little, since by then the Company was too involved in the negotiations with Canada and realized that it could gain more from the new dominion than from the United States. Slowly but steadily, the processes of Victorian law-making moved towards an arrangement between the Company and Canada. Both Canada and Britain, which wished to withdraw its military forces from North America, realized that if British Columbia on the Pacific Coast were to be included in a Canadian union, Canada would have to govern the prairies. Besides, even the Hudson's Bay Company was convinced that chartered companies were hopelessly out of date in the nineteenth century, with political democracy and free trade important issues.

When the British North America Act of 1867 established Canada as a self-governing dominion, it was no surprise that Rupert's Land and the Northwest Territories were to be admitted to the new confederation. The following year, by the Rupert's Land Act, the British government was specifically authorized "to accept a surrender upon terms" of the Company's lands and to arrange for them to be admitted into the Dominion of Canada. Neither of these acts placed any express obligation on the Hudson's Bay Company, but it was understood that refusal to comply would result in the government's refusal to renew the Company's license.

Yet an agreement was not reached for some time. The Canadians wanted to sign a general accord and work out the conditions later. But the Company, having waited more than twenty years for the American government to settle its claims under the Oregon agreement, had no intention of accepting generalities. The whole winter of 1868–69 was spent in negotiating all the details, and in March of the latter year a "deed of surrender" was signed.

The Canadian government was to make a token payment of three hundred thousand pounds. More important were the concessions of land. The Company retained some forty-five thousand acres around its 120 posts, and some of this land was to become very valuable since it lay on the sites of future cities like Winnipeg, Edmonton, and Victoria. Most important, the Company was entitled to claim one-twentieth of the land laid out for settlement during the next fifty years in what was called the Fertile Belt, the area east of the Rockies between the North Saskatchewan River and the United States border. Under this clause, the Company eventually sold seven million acres of prairie farm land. Finally, though the monopoly would end, the Company was free to trade wherever it wished in Canada, and it was specifically protected against "exceptional taxes."

So, with a very satisfactory agreement for its financier owners, the Company passed into a new era. It was no longer a sovereign entity, ruling unchallenged over millions of square miles of land but neither was it an outdated monopoly.

Yet the Company's sovereignty did not come to an end quietly or undramatically. Under the agreement, the surrender would take effect in November, 1869, when the Canadian sovereignty over Rupert's Land and the Northwest would be proclaimed. But the transfer did not take place when planned.

When news of the deed of surrender reached the Red River, the few recent Canadian immigrants from Ontario were elated. The older settlers—the *métis* and the English-speaking half-breeds—were unhappy because no provision had been made for their rights. Their fears seemed confirmed when the new coalition government of Sir John A. Macdonald in Ottawa passed legislation to govern the territory as soon as the surrender came into effect. The proposed new government was the same kind of rule, by a governor with a council appointed for outside, against which the Canadians themselves had rebelled in the 1830s.

It was the *métis* who took the initiative of resistance, largely as the result of a series of precipitate actions by the Canadian authorities, especially William McDougall, a pompous and devious demagogue who was minister of public works in the Macdonald administration.

In September, 1868, six months before the surrender was negotiated, McDougall sent a government contractor to build a road from the Red River to Ontario—a case of trespassing which was carried out despite weak protests from the Company's dying governor, William McTavish. Then, in October, 1869, while the actual transfer of government lay ahead, McDougall—with the Ottawa cabinet's consent —instructed Colonel J. S. Dennis to begin a general survey of the Red River settlement.

The survey, undertaken by Canadian officials in what was still legally non-Canadian territory, was the immediate cause of the Red River uprising. The *métis* had occupied the land as squatters, and they were afraid the vagueness of their titles would be used to drive them from their farms. It was at this point that Louis Riel, the son of Jean-Louis Riel, who had defied the Company in 1849, appeared as their leader. He was an intelligent, strong-willed, and educated young man of twenty-five.

Since the Hudson's Bay governor and council of Assiniboia were either powerless or unwilling to take action, Riel decided the *métis* must act for themselves. On October 11, while the surveyors were on the land of his cousin André Nault, he appeared with a small band of men and disrupted the survey by jumping on the measuring chain. This small act was the beginning of Riel's career as a rebel.

Immediately afterwards, news reached Fort Garry that, after annexation, the first Canadian lieutenant governor would be the very William McDougall who had been responsible for the territorial infringement. McDougall was instructed to set off at once for the Red River, to supervise the transfer of territory when the royal proclamation was issued.

Ignoring the inert and discredited council of Assiniboia, a hastily convened assembly of the *métis* elected a National Committee, with Riel as secretary; and the committee, in its turn, decided that McDougall must be kept out of the territory as the only means of assuring that the settlers' grievances were heard before Canadian authority was established. Immediate action followed. At Pembina a courier handed McDougall a message from Riel, warning him not to enter the territory without the committee's permission. The warning was backed by a company of armed *métis* deployed across the trail leading to Fort Garry. After sending some officers to investigate, McDougall decided to stay in Pembina.

Meanwhile, the Canadians on the Red River were making the tension worse. Colonel Dennis tried to raise a force to escort McDougall into the territory. His efforts were unsuccessful, but they roused Riel's apprehensions, and on November 2, the *métis* seized the Hudson's Bay headquarters of Fort Garry, with its arms, munition, and stores. The fort henceforth became the center of their activities, garrisoned by buffalo hunters who maintained an astonishing discipline.

With the seizure of Fort Garry, the last vestige of Hudson's Bay authority vanished; and the National Committee of the *métis* emerged as the sole political force on the Red

River. It could hardly be said that the *métis* were in rebellion against constituted authority, since Canada had no rights yet over the Northwest, and the Hudson's Bay officers had virtually abdicated through inaction. Riel always maintained that his loyalty to Queen Victoria had never wavered. But he recognized the need to reinforce the appearance of legality, and he was anxious for wider support. Three days after seizing Fort Garry he appealed to the English-speaking settlers to cooperate in a joint council. These settlers realized that the issues affected everyone along the Red River; and every parish sent its delegates to the first meeting of the joint council.

Almost the only significant act of this body was to draw up a list of rights, demanding popular representation and local autonomy before the territory was ceded to the dominion. Had the Canadian government been willing to negotiate on the basis of the list, more violent phases of the Red River Rising might have been avoided. This, however, did not suit McDougall's ambition, and, since the royal proclamation had not yet been issued, he forged one. Next he authorized Colonel Dennis to disperse the insurgents by force.

Having crossed into the Red River settlement, Dennis tried to raise a force of English-speaking settlers to oppose Riel but only a few answered his call. And contrary to his orders, they barricaded themselves in a house near Fort Garry. Riel brought out cannon and laid siege to the house; when its forty-five defenders surrendered, they were imprisoned.

The actions of McDougall and Dennis were disowned as illegal by the Canadian Cabinet; and McDougall abandoned his adventure and returned home. But by then it was too late: Riel and the Canadian immigrants had been driven into more extreme positions.

Riel, now president of the National Committee, became increasingly dictatorial. Canadian sympathizers were arrested; the Hudson's Bay Company's safe was rifled to pay the *métis* guards; the local newspapers were suppressed. Finally, in January, 1870, with the reluctant consent of William McTavish, the ailing Company governor, a provisional government was formed, with Riel at its head.

A few days later a party of armed Canadian immigrants marched in from the village of Portage la Prairie, sixty miles west on the Assiniboine, to rescue the prisoners held in Fort Garry. Riel released the prisoners and the Portage men then agreed to disperse. But when a group of them marched past Fort Garry, Riel's men captured them.

Riel now acted with inexplicable and tragic violence. He threatened to shoot Captain Bolton, the leader of the insurgents. Then, having spared Bolton, he insisted on court-martialing another ringleader, Thomas Scott. Scott was a hot-tempered Orangeman who had been involved in several violent incidents since his arrival on the Red River; and he was certainly one of the most prejudiced anti-Catholics among the Canadian immigrants. But the charge of treason, which Riel brought against him, was flimsy, and his execution, on the morning after his trial, was as unjustified as it was unwise.

Meanwhile, the withdrawal of the unfortunate McDougall was followed by the arrival of more tactful delegates from Canada. The most important were Alexandre Taché, the local Roman Catholic Bishop, and Donald A. Smith. Smith was general manager of the Montreal district of the Hudson's Bay Company, and he had been picked by Sir

John A. Macdonald because of his experience. Smith had never been to the Red River, but he was an astute man with an eye for his own interests as well as the Company's. His aim was to succeed in his mission so as to make the Canadian government indebted to the Company whose rule over the West it was replacing.

Smith succeeded in allaying Riel's suspicions, and he personally assured the settlers that the Canadian government now recognized the necessity of making concessions to them. At the end of March, as a result of his intervention and Bishop Taché's, the people of the Red River sent Father Richot and Alfred H. Scott as their delegates to present the list of rights. It seemed as though the peaceful integration of the Northwest into Canada was assured at last.

But by now the execution of Scott had become a major issue in Upper Canada. The Orange lodges led a campaign for vengeance on Scott's killers; and the public fury, whipped up by local demagogues, was so great that the Red River delegates were arrested for murder on their arrival in the capital, though neither of them had been remotely connected with Scott's execution. They were released in time to witness the passing of the Manitoba Act, by which the insurgents on the Red River gained almost all they had demanded. Their territory was absorbed by Canada as a province—named Manitoba—with local self-government. At last the surrender could take place, and the Hudson's Bay Company officially transferred its powers to the Dominion of Canada on July 15, 1870, just over two hundred years after Charles II had made the original Adventurers "Lordes and Proprietors" of the vast spaces of Rupert's Land.

Even then, the actual transfer was not made immediately. Riel remained as head of the provisional government until

Colonel Garnet Wolseley, a British officer, was sent to the Red River at the head of an expeditionary force of British regulars and Canadian militia. Riel had been promised an amnesty but, learning that the government had reneged, he fled to the United States. Riel remained in exile until he returned in 1885 to head a second rebellion of the *métis* in the present province of Saskatchewan.

The last governor in Rupert's Land, William MacTavish, had already departed for England, but Donald Smith remained to represent the Company. Colonel Wolseley asked him to continue governing until the Canadian lieutenant governor arrived. On September 2 lieutenant governor A. G. Archibald finally set foot in the Red River valley. This was another triumph for the *métis*, for Archibald, a man of liberal sentiments, had a great sympathy for the *métis*. It was to him that Donald Smith surrendered the sovereign powers granted by Charles II in 1670. "I yield up my responsibilities with pleasure," Smith remarked. "I do not anticipate much pleasure on my own account," Archibald is said to have replied.

As a final twist, in the elections to the provincial legislature in December, 1870, one of the successful candidates was Donald Smith, then in charge of the Company's affairs in the whole of Canada. Since the old title of governor had been abolished, Smith was the first of the Company's chief commissioners, charged with the task of seeing that, despite the loss of political power, the Company's economic empire did not perish.

Epilogue

Three hundred years ago the *Nonsuch* sailed back from Hudson's Bay with its cargo of furs, and King Charles signed the charter that established the Hudson's Bay Company. A hundred years ago the Company gave up its territorial sovereignty and its trading monopoly. Yet today the Company prospers more than ever as the oldest mercantile corporation in the world.

The Company's past lingers on in some ways. All changes in its constitution are submitted to the crown for ratification by royal charter. It retains the resounding name conferred in the original charter; its shareholders can still flatter themselves with the title of Adventurers; and its annual gathering, at Beaver Hall in London, is still a general court and not a general meeting.

All of the other chartered companies—the great East India Company, the Turkey Company, the Africa Company, the Virginia Company, the Company of Merchant Adventurers—are mere memories, living in history. The Hudson's Bay Company alone has survived, through an almost miraculous adaptability. The other chartered companies had ossified under their monopolies, and when the monopolies were abolished they could not adapt to new conditions. The Hudson's Bay Company had been tempered in the great struggle with the North Westers, so that the united Company which Simpson reshaped was in splendid commercial form. The transfer of ownership in 1863 brought a vigorous group of financiers who managed their investments wisely. Finally, in Donald Smith, who later became Lord Strathcona and one of the architects of modern Canada, they had a chief commissioner who was as alive to new possibilities as Simpson had been in his time.

Today the Hudson's Bay Company presents two sides to the world. It is still the world's most important fur dealer. Through its auction rooms in London, New York, and Montreal, more than a hundred million dollars worth of skins pass every year, while it operates two hundred posts scattered in tiny communities across the vast North. At the same time it operates a chain of more than thirty modern department stores in cities across Canada. Its total receipts each year run to more than half a billion dollars—a long way from the thirteen hundred pounds (then about seven thousand dollars) fetched by the *Nonsuch*'s first cargo. And its thirty thousand shareholders are a far cry from the eighteen gentlemen—some very reluctant—who put up money for the first venture in 1668.

The Hudson's Bay Company survived and prospered because it rode with the current of history. In the late nineteenth century, though the influx of settlers in the West swept away its exclusive privileges, the Company was left with an advantage. It was first in the field to reap the rewards of change.

The settlement of the West took place in stages. First, during the 1870s, there was an influx from Eastern Canada into the new province of Manitoba. Then, in the 1880s and 1890s, immigrants from Britain and from eastern and central Europe began to flood over the so-called Fertile Belt, in the southern prairies, where the Hudson's Bay Company had land rights. Towards the end of 1890 and early in the twentieth century, quick-growing strains of wheat were developed, and a new influx of immigrants began filling the northern prairies and the Peace River district. But the vast area of forests and tundra to the north remained the special domain of the fur trader.

But the fur trade had also succumbed to change. The revolution in transportation eventually reached the remote wilderness. The great change was in the transportation axis between Hudson's Bay and the Red River.

Up to the late 1850s the water route through the Bay was the most expeditious way of serving the posts in the western interior. By 1858 the railways had reached Minnesota, and a new route was developed. Red River carts transported supplies over a trail leading from Fort Garry to railhead in American territory. In 1859 the Company introduced the first steamboat on the Red River, and by 1868, the brigades from Athabaska and the Mackenzie were coming to Fort Garry instead of York Factory, to link up with the steamboat and railway. In 1871, the steamboats replaced the brigades. By 1874 steamboats were operating on the Saskatchewan River, and by 1877 the first of them reached Edmonton. This was the end of the voyageurs, and hundreds of Indians and *métis* were sent back to trapping and hunting. By 1875 York Factory's preeminence had vanished; the interior trade was centered on Fort Garry, and York Factory was left with the coastal trade on the Bay.

The old sea route, once the Company's great pride, fell largely into disuse.

Many years later, however, there was a great revival of trading beside the northern seas. When Arctic furs, particularly fox, became the fashion, the Company established a series of forts among the channels and islands of the Arctic. By World War I posts had been set up at the mouth of the Mackenzie, on Baffin Island, and on Victoria Island. The Company's expansion did not go unchallenged. A number of smaller companies, of which the most active was the Paris firm of Revillon Frères, were operating in the region. Eventually, though, the Company swallowed up its competitors and today, in most communities in the far North, it enjoys a monopoly in fact if not in law.

Until little more than a decade ago, the posts were simple log buildings where the Eskimos and northern Indians traded their furs for the Company's metal tokens, which they exchanged for goods. The traditional exchange of furs against manufactured goods was still the basis of the trade. But there has been an extraordinary change in the last few years.

A social revolution is taking place in the Canadian North. The government has intervened with welfare programs, industrial projects, construction works, and the native peoples of the North now have more cash than they had ever handled before. Today the Hudson's Bay posts, even those on the bleak shores of Baffin Island or in the Barren Land, have become miniature department stores, supplying a great variety of sophisticated commodities as well as traditional items like snow knives and ice chisels.

Only one-eighth of the Company's present trade in the northern stores is in furs; nowadays most of its furs are

ranch-grown. But some of the old features of the trade remain. At the Arctic posts, merchandise still arrives only once
a year, by the annual ship whose arrival is a major event.
But the old isolation has given way to the bush plane and
the short-wave radio, and the old self-contained life of the
trades is a receding memory. Nevertheless, the Company
remains one of the dominant elements in the life of the land
that stretches beyond the edges of cultivation to the
margins of the permanent ice.

South of the sub-Arctic, and in the states over the border
that once formed part of the Oregon Territory, the influence of the Hudson's Bay Company is not so pervasive.
But it is reflected in the patterns of settlement and even in
the boundaries on the map. Many cities and towns are on
sites first chosen as forts by the Hudson's Bay or North
West Company. These include no less than three capitals
of Canadian provinces: Winnipeg in Manitoba, Edmonton
in Alberta, and Victoria in British Columbia, as well as
American towns like Spokane, Walla Walla, Boise, and
Vancouver, Washington. The great highways through the
West often follow the trails used by the fur traders, and
sometimes the railways go through mountain passes discovered by fur-trading explorers. The maps in use today are
based on information first collected by explorers like Alexander Mackenzie, David Thompson, Samuel Hearne,
and John Rae. Nowhere, from the Great Lakes westward,
is it possible to ignore the mark which the Company left
on the land.

After the transfer of power to Canada in 1870, the Company realistically expected the fur trade to dwindle wherever settlement took place. In 1871 a proposal was actually

put forward to abandon the fur trade completely, but instead a policy of cutting transportation costs was adopted, and the trade survived. At the same time, speculation in land values became an important part of Company policy, and continued to be so until the end of the 1950s. During the early 1880s, and again from 1906 to 1919, profits from this source were enormous, and for the first time dividends equaled those declared in the 1680s—45 per cent in 1906, 50 per cent in 1913, 40 per cent in 1918, and 45 per cent again in 1919. In years like these, receipts from land sales ran into millions of dollars, far exceeding any profits in the past from the fur trade.

The land sales policy of the Company was shaped by Donald Smith. Between 1870 and 1874 Smith held the positions of chief commissioner and land commissioner. In 1874 he relinquished the chief commissionership, which related mainly to the fur trade, but remained land commissioner until 1879. This fitted his personal interests, for he was much alive to the prospects of achieving fortune and power through developing the prairies, and he was already involved in railway developments in Minnesota. When the Canadian Pacific Railway was being planned Smith was among its originators. No one has yet untangled the links between the Hudson's Bay Company and the railway interests of the time, but it is significant that Charles J. Brydges, who succeeded Smith as the Company's land commissioner in 1879, was a railway speculator, while Sandford Fleming, the engineer who planned the Canadian Pacific Railway, became a member of the Company's committee in 1882. Smith helped the Canadian Pacific with timely loans during its construction, and he was chosen to drive the last spike in 1885. By then he had also been a member of the Company's committee for two years; and in 1889 he became its director. The Canadian Pacific Railway and the Hudson's Bay Company both prospered by selling land to the immigrants, and their interlocking directorates suggest that they worked together.

The business of selling land was chancy. The early 1880s was a time of great profits, and the late 1880s a time of recession when the shareholders had to go without dividends. The fur trade remained relatively stable, but even in good years brought in only a fraction of the profits from land sales during the boom. This new financial conformation of the company—partly speculative real estate corporation and partly solid fur business—necessarily brought about changes in its constitution.

In the new situation, the wintering partnership began to look anachronistic. As the fur trade diminished in importance, the conflict between the wintering partners and the shareholders grew worse. The winterers still maintained that their deed poll entitled them to share in all the Company's profits, while the committee in London argued that they were entitled only to a share of the income from furs, which was dwindling. Twenty years of dispute followed, but the committee had the advantage, since it appointed all new officers on a salaried basis, and by 1893, an agreement was worked out with the surviving winterers and the deed poll was abolished. From then on, all the Company's officers were salaried employees, and the Company was reorganized as a joint-stock enterprise.

The era of land speculation was a passing—though very profitable—phase for the Hudson's Bay Company. As early as 1906, seeing the Company's millions of acres rapidly melting away, Strathcona had restricted sales so that land could fetch greater profits. By the early 1920s, most of the good land had been sold, and the Company's reserves were used to build up its present great retail business.

The Company's retail business reaches back to 1830, when a store was established at Fort Garry on the Red River. It remained an unambitious venture, carried on in a small log building in a corner of the compound. The Company did not enter the retail business seriously until the Fraser gold rush, when it opened a large store in Victoria. Another large store was set up in Winnipeg during the 1860s, and in 1871 the Company decided to build up a chain of stores. As the farmers moved across the country, the Company moved with them. Stores were opened at Portage la Prairie, at Calgary, at Edmonton, later at Saskatoon and Regina. In Vancouver the Hudson's Bay Company moved in during 1887, the very year the first rough buildings went up on the site of Canada's western metropolis.

But these were pioneer stores, selling simple goods needed by the first settlers. By 1910 the westerners had become more sophisticated in their demands, and the policy of building large department stores was launched. During the next twenty years the great rectangular blocks of the Hudson's Bay stores became familiar sights in Canadian cities from Winnipeg westward. By 1960 an eastern chain of department stores was bought up, and now the Hudson's Bay Company's trade stretches across the continent from St. John's, Newfoundland, to Victoria on Vancouver Island, a distance of about four thousand miles, and from Sarnia in Ontario more than two thousand miles northward to Arctic Bay on the farthest shore of Baffin Island.

The Hudson's Bay Company was the one chartered company that refused to die. It survived to play its part in the building of Canada, and today, like the Canadian Pacific Railway, the Royal Canadian Mounted Police, it is one of those institutions that Canadians can criticize but never dismiss. But its historical importance is wider than Canada, for it represents one of the great forces in the drive that impelled Americans and Canadians alike across the great plains and the mountains towards the western ocean.

Further Reading

The classic book on the Hudson's Bay Company is E. E. Rich's
History of the Hudson's Bay Company, 1670–1870 (2 volumes),
published by the Hudson's Bay Record Society in London,
1958–59. The Hudson's Bay Record Society has also published
a valuable series of reprinted documents from the early days of
the Company. A much shorter and more popular book, *The
Honourable Company*, by Douglas McKay (New York, 1936),
surveys the subject up to the 1930's; a later paperback edition,
published in Toronto in 1966, carries the story rather lightly
up to that date. There is, however, no complete history of the
last hundred years of the Company, though much material is
to be found in articles printed in *The Beaver*, a highly interest-
ing magazine published quarterly by the Company.

The Fur Trade in Canada by Harold F. Innis (Yale, 1930)
fills in the economic background to the Company's activities,
and a useful digest of the travels of the fur traders is John
Warkentin's *The Western Interior of Canada: A Record of
Geographical Discovery, 1612–1917* (Toronto, 1964). Of the
individual narratives of Hudson's Bay Company explorers the
best is Samuel Hearne's *Journey to the Northern Ocean*, reprinted in Toronto in 1958. The stories of two great fur
traders are told well in *Alexander Mackenzie and the Northwest* by Roy Daniells (London, 1969) and *McGillivray: Lord
of the Northwest* by Marjorie W. Campbell (Toronto, 1962),
whose *The Northwest Company* (Toronto, 1957) is the best

account of its subject. On the first settlement of the Red River Valley, which led up to the last decisive struggle between the Hudson's Bay Company and the North West Company, the best account is *Lord Selkirk of Red River* by John M. Gray (Toronto, 1963), while an excellent narrative of the events in the same region that attended the end of the Company's rule as a territorial empire in 1870 is George F. G. Stanley's *Louis Riel* (Toronto, 1963).

Index